Indoor Gardens

INDOOR

GARDENS

by Ware Budlong

Hawthorn Books   Publishers   New York

INDOOR GARDENS

First Edition: 1967

5080

Contents

List of Illustrations

My appreciation to

Ruth Aley, my literary agent, for most helpful interest in the writing of this book

Paul Arnold, International Registrar for the Gesneriaceae (excluding *Saintpaulia*), for suggestions of some of the plants mentioned in the chapter on gesneriad gardens and also for reading that chapter for criticism

Ted Budlong, my son, for taking over half the photographs used as illustrations, and also making the two terrariums and the planters for rock garden and waterfall garden

Elizabeth C. Hall, Associate Curator of Education, the New York Botanical Garden, for reading the book for criticism

Bobs Pinkerton, specialist in herbs as well as editing, for suggestions for the chapter on herb gardens

Alice Ramsey, illustrator and portraitist, for the sketch used as a motif

All the photographs in this book illustrate gardens designed and constructed by the author.

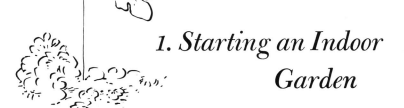

1. Starting an Indoor Garden

INDOOR GARDENS ARE NOT MERELY DWARF COPIES OF OUTDOOR gardens. They have attractions very much their own.

An indoor garden may be a miniature landscape, alive and changing, with its hills and trees and flowers. Or again, it may be no larger than one's hands, with three plants that belong together in a container that belongs to the room.

Choosing the garden you want is fun in itself, whether you decide on tropical flowers blooming while snow drifts against the windows, or tall greenery in a room divider, or a grouping of miniature plants as tiny as finger rings. Planting is a further pleasure, as the arrangement builds. And there is always an accent of surprise in the final effect, because indoor gardens bring their own personalities to a room.

Interest in them may arrive overnight, or progress through the years. My own interest began when I was quite young. In other houses, I might see a fern in a pot, or flowers in a medley of pots jostling each other on a plant stand, or a row of plants in red clay pots straggling along a windowsill. But in our house were the gardens. Gardens with tiny plants in a landscape, gardens with larger flowering plants, and always a wild garden full of familiar things from the woods and lake shore.

At first I merely looked at them and watched the progress of berries and flowers. Then they took on importance. Perhaps the miniature landscape caught at a child's interest in child-sized things, or perhaps the wild garden had a carry-over of lake and woods. Certainly my mother's interest had its own quiet contagion. Anyway, I was fairly caught, and by the time I was six I wanted an indoor garden of my own.

Of course I had to progress by stages. Spotting plants in the woods that looked like those in the wildflower garden at home; then learning that the transplanting of wild plants was quite a different matter from handling the young marigolds I had been allowed to set out in a flower bed; finally finding out how plants would settle down contentedly indoors. But with set-backs of impatience, I finally arrived at my indoor garden, which was a mixture of hardy wild plants and good-natured ones from the outdoor garden, and had no plan or design that I can remember, but was my own and valued accordingly.

From that time on indoor gardens were part of a proper life. Whether coping with the winter climate of a New York apartment, learning the possibilities of Florida gardening when I lived there for several years, or adapting indoor gardens to a variety of northern suburban houses, I found my interest holding and deepening. In interim periods when demands conflicted, there were bleak places about the house where gardens should have been. And when the gardens were back, the house was right again.

For those who have gardened out of doors, the shift to indoor gardening is an easy bridging. For those who are used to the pleasant but often haphazard business of house plants, indoor gardens have the added values of design, creating a special effect, accenting the decor of a room, and finding that to add two and two plants together in a garden can make a unit which is far more interesting than four plants in separate pots.

There also are variegated rewards for those who have not had much to do with flowering or foliage plants before start-

ing an indoor garden. Information about plants and their culture can be gathered along the way, with no expertise necessary at the start.

Some of the gardens in this book are planned for the inex-
perienced gardener, and some accommodating plants are suggested. And as one garden leads to another, knowledge will
stockpile, so that more unusual gardens will follow. Other
gardens suggested here need more attention to specific points
of culture. The different gardens may be leafed through to find
one that fits an interest or a location—perhaps a waterfall
garden, a gesneriad garden, a wind-chime garden for a child's
room.

For a first-time indoor garden, the steps are easy. Choice of
a container should be the start, according to the type of garden
planned: a large planter with slanting sides for a rock garden,
for example, or a smaller one for a movable garden that will be
sometimes in a sunny window and sometimes on the coffee
table. Suggestions for planters will be found in following chapters.

A walk through nursery greenhouses gives a chance for personal selection of flowering and foliage plants. Further plants
to fit a special design can be ordered by mail. City florists often
have plants that will suit a garden plan, and useful plants turn
up at the five-and-ten.

For soil, a variety of mixtures are on the market, sifted and
sterilized, ready for the special aspects of apartment living and
simplified gardening. The combining in a single garden of two
plants which need different types of soil is accomplished by
use of an insulating wall below ground; this can be made of
pieces of slate from the discards lying around the yard of a
supplier to contractors, or of flat pieces of rock, or folds of
heavy foil.

Other points of plant needs are as simple. For light, there
is the choice of a sunny window, the suggestions for a no-sun
room, the use of fluorescent lighting. A hospitable temperature
for plants is arrived at by watching the thermostat and giving
up an overheated room in winter. Humidity needs are met with
devices ranging from a portable humidifier to a water-container

Figure 1

Ted Budlong

Maidenhair fern, in an old English bowl of maidenhair fern pattern, as described in Chapter six.

from the hardware store that can be hung behind a radiator, and pebble-and-water trays. Proper watering merely means noting the needs of selected plants, and checking regularly that the soil is correctly moist. It is not necessary to mist plants with a fine spray, though some of them, maidenhair fern for example, would appreciate this (Figure 1).

Feeding of plants is simplified by commercial fertilizers, with information noted on their labels, the easiest being the concentrates that are to be added to water. Further details of care, valuable for instance in specialization, and ranging from ordinary routine to remedies for occasional pests, are found in cultural handbooks. Different points of culture are taken up in succeeding chapters, sometimes with application to certain plants, sometimes in reference to specific gardens.

The planting of the first garden not only is a pleasure, but starts an association with the plants that may be objective interest or a more personal relationship. Either way, this leads to interest in caring for the plants, which is highlighted by their response.

One aspect of indoor gardening may seem a fringe matter, but bits of the fringe keep getting into the gardens. So it is mentioned here in some detail. This is the use of botanical names.

There are obvious values. The use of a botanical name identifies a plant with accuracy, whereas the common names of some plants overlap confusingly. It is of value also in selecting plants from a catalog and ordering them. For those who wish to correspond with growers in other countries, it offers a universal language for referring to plants. Scientific names of plants follow rules under the international codes of nomenclature, in a system of naming that originated with Linnaeus in the eighteenth century.

On the other hand, a barrage of lengthy scientific names is not the easiest beginning. Also, botanical names are sometimes used in conversation for mixed purposes. This can be a status thing, a person's claim to belong to an in-group. It can be a subjective pleasure, carried to the point of refusing to use common names.

A compromise is suggested for the beginner: note the botanical names of only two or three plants, the ones most important in a garden, or those which may be the start of specialization; then add further scientific names for use, only as fast as it can be done without boredom or irritation. With a widening interest in indoor gardens, there may come along a corresponding interest in technical names.

And a side suggestion: use botanical names in conversation with a kindly spirit. When a friend who knows nothing about plants looks at one of them and asks, "What is that cute little flower?" it is daunting for him to get a complicated answer in Latin. He is apt to say, "Oh," and change the subject, with a resolve to let horticulture alone in the future. Much better to swallow one's reaction to the word "cute," and answer with a common name if there is one, or say, "It has a long name—so-and-so—but it does have a nice color, doesn't it," which gives the friend something to catch hold of.

To those who already know the pleasures of indoor gardens, details of these pleasures are redundant. But for many, gardens are still to be started. An indoor garden may be as different from an assortment of house plants in pots, as a complete painting is different from detail studies of small areas in it. With a garden, one is concerned with an aesthetic whole, toward which color harmony and contrast, details of balance and asymmetry, and the complete design all contribute. The indoor garden can be focused self-expression, an experiment for a new effect, or—to scrape the moss off an old phrase—it can be just a garden-variety of fun.

2. Waterfall Gardens

AN INDOOR GARDEN WITH A WATERFALL HAS A SPECIAL PERSON-
ality, part the play of light on moving water, part the rippling,
splashing sound; more than these, a sense of something busy
and self-absorbed, set apart in its own place. The small size of
the falls and the fact of having a waterfall in one's own room
also give a quality different from full-sized falls out of doors.

This garden may feature the falls, using much of the space
for them and a pool, or may half conceal the water with plants
and flowers. The waterfall may be a simple straight drop over
rocks, or wander slanting down the garden slope.

Size of the planter should be decided first, according to the
space where it will stand. The high back of the planter is the
governing factor, with the other measurements proportional.

The planter shown in Figure 3 is medium sized, the back
rising sixteen inches. The waterfall emerges from rocks at the
top of the hill, toward the right; slants down to eddy in a small
pool; slants down again to fall into a larger pool.

The mechanics of the waterfall are simple. A small electric
pump, available from Arthur Eames Allgrove (see suppliers'
listing), rests on a table behind or below the garden. The pump

sends a flow of water through plastic tubing, entering the garden by a hole in the back of the planter near the head of the falls. After passing down the falls and into the pool, the water exits through a plastic tube in the bottom of the pool which passes through another hole at the planter back, and into a large high pan—in which sits the pump, busily recirculating this water up again to the falls.

With the pump come directions as to the tubing to be used, which can be purchased at an auto-supply store. A length of ordinary electric lamp cord from a hardware store is stripped at one end and attached to the terminals of the pump, with electrical tape used to finish the joining. A clip-on plug is put on the wire's other end, to be plugged into an ordinary wall socket with no transformer needed. A switch can be incorporated easily into the cord, or a cord can be chosen with switch attached, so that the waterfall can be turned on inconspicuously.

This small pump provides an adequate flow of water to the falls. The rate of flow is adjusted by changing the height of the pump—the lower the pump (on the next shelf down or on a lower table, for example), the slower the flow. The water level in the pan should be maintained at the maximum directed by the accompanying instructions, and the pan in which the pump rests should be large enough to allow an adequate water supply.

Purchases for the garden, aside from planting, include the motor, which costs under ten dollars, lumber for the planter, the plastic tubing and electric cord, cement for the pool, a pan to hold the water supply, if none is available around the house. The length of the tubing will depend on where the pan is set, perhaps on a table behind the planter. In the illustration, the pan and motor are behind the curtain on a cupboard shelf.

The planter is made from half-inch plywood—and be sure to specify external, or outdoor, plywood at your lumberyard, to stand up well against rot. Have it cut as follows:

1 piece 6" x 24" for the front
1 piece 16" x 24" for the back

2 pieces 17″ x 16″ for the sides
1 piece 18″ x 24″ for the bottom

The side pieces should be cut diagonally as shown by the dotted line in sketch A of Figure 2 to form a trapezoid. The pieces should all be stained and after drying should be put together with glue and nails as in sketch B.

An extra step will add polish to your planter: this is to put veneer on the visible edges of the plywood. This is not nearly as

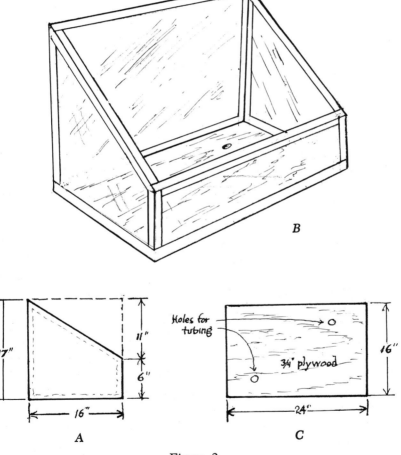

B

A

Holes for tubing

¾″ plywood

17″

11″

6″

16″

16″

24″

C

Figure 2

hard as it sounds, for real-wood veneer is available in rolled strips like tape. Get veneer of the same shade as the plywood, such as fir, in half-inch size or larger, and trim to size. Cut four lengths to fit the top edges of the front, back, and sides of the planter, and one length to cover the edge of the bottom visible at the front. Glue the strips to the edges with a strong glue such as epoxy, and then stain them with the same stain used for the rest of the planter.

Before assembling, drill two holes in the back of the planter for the water tubing to enter and leave, as shown in sketch C. Position of these holes is planned for a slanting waterfall leading to the pool at the lower left. For a straight fall of water, the top hole would be directly over the bottom one.

The size and shape of the pool are a matter of personal choice. The pool is easily made. The one in the illustration is cement, with the surface casually rough, and the color toning in with nearby rocks. Having decided on this material to make a natural effect with the rocks, I used Sakrete, a mixture of sand and Portland cement which only needs the addition of water. I partly filled a box with sand, and hollowed the sand out in the shape of the pool I wanted, allowing for over an inch thickness of cement. Into this mold I spread the cement, which had been mixed and stirred like batter to a thickness that would hold its position. Through the bottom of the cement shape ran the end of the plastic tube that would take the water off eventually, its opening covered with foil so no cement could enter. While the cement shape was still damp, I roughened any surface that looked too smoothly artificial.

For long use, the planter should be coated inside with rot preventative, as mentioned in Chapter 9. The pool can also be painted on the inside with battleship-gray floor enamel, which is sold for use on cement, and is not noticeable after it is dry. Before painting, you should check the pool to make sure it is watertight around the plastic tube, and if not it should be caulked there.

Planning the waterfall is more fun if it is done with rocks, laying them out in different positions to get an interesting and natural effect. When the design is decided, the rocks are

cemented together with Sakrete, so no water will seep through
later into the soil, and also painted the same blending gray.
Use of rocks that are much the same color as the dried cement
makes a natural effect easier. They can be brought together
to make a V-shaped channel for the water, or fastened against
a flat rock for a base, as illustrated. This water-course of rocks,
all in one piece finally, will lie against the garden hill. If the
pool is set in position in the garden soil, near the front of the
planter, the arrangement of rocks can be tried out, with water
streaming down into the pool, before it is cemented to the pool
at its foot. The two main things to consider are, first, the
water channel—from the source through the top plastic tube
concealed by rocks, down the falls to the pool, with the rocks
placed to catch the water and send it on down in the direction
desired—and second, a natural look for the rocks, with space
allowed beside them for vines and ferns that will spread across
them later.

The hill is built up from the flat foreground with its pool,
as described for rock gardens in Chapter 8. Down underneath,
among the drainage pebbles, runs the plastic tube that carries
off water from the pool, through the outlet hole at the lower
back of the planter. The hill can rise steeply at one side, with
a rock retaining wall to be used later for a cascade of vines,
and the other side showing a more gradual slope with the
rocks that hold the earth concealed for the most part. The
shape of the hill depends on where the waterfall is placed, and
whether it wanders across the garden or falls straight down.
After the rock composition for the water channel is in place
against slanting earth, the rest of the hill can be worked out
to conform. Pockets of space are provided for ferns and plants
that will need good root room. Space is planned near the top
for vines and small plants.

If rocks are featured in the garden, there should be quite a
few small plants and vines used, to give a tracery of green
against them. Larger plants can be used, both foliage and
flowering plants, as long as they don't throw the waterfall out
of proportion.

A waterfall garden planted entirely with ferns and vines

would have an interesting design. Or all the planting could be done with material collected in the woods and countryside, or with wildflowers and plants ordered as mentioned in Chapter 5.

Moss can be used around the pool, with vines trailing across the edge. Fern fronds can curve over it. A flat piece of lichened rock can extend out at one side, concealing the plastic tip where water drains out the bottom.

As the planting continues, different effects can be tried: a mass of vines curving around a rock, plants of varying height to give contrast, patterned foliage. Pockets can be made for bromeliads, with foil pierced with drainage holes and filled with sphagnum moss or osmunda. Sooner or later there will be one right place for a miniature tree, or a gesneriad with unusual foliage, or the special fern that needs space to show its pattern.

From time to time you may want to change the foliage plants, use new vines, add flowering plants you have grown from seed. The garden may alter from month to month as you want a new effect. But always there will be the waterfall, busy with its own enchantment among the vines and leaves.

Figure 3

Ira Finke

The waterfall in this garden starts under vines, the source concealed by a jut of rock. The water swirls down against other rocks that change its direction, to reach the pool at the lower left. Over thirty plants live among the rocks, climb up and down, spread across the rim of the pool.

Figure 4

Ira Finke

The room divider is planted here to rise gradually toward the back. Trailing down at the front, in flower, is Columnea *'Yellow Dragon,' with the white flowers of* Sinningia speciosa *lifting above. A bromeliad,* Billbergia braziliense zebrina *with its crossbanded leaves, is next. Grape ivy rises higher toward the center. Still taller is the mistletoe fig, its berries showing high at the left. A Christmas fern spreads fronds at the back of the planter. On the flat space of the divider, next to the wall, is a green glass vase holding sprays of eucalyptus.*

3. Garden Decor

PLANTS HAVE BEEN GROWN IN THE HOUSE SINCE ANCIENT TIMES, but in recent years there has been a wider tide of green indoors. Vines, foliage, and flowering plants are found more often nowadays in apartments and private houses as well as in offices, though they are not always used to full advantage for the decor and architecture of a room.

Too often a casual effect is offered by a stolid plant in a stolid pot; a more stylized effect is made by an urn with a bark-covered post or slab of wood set in it, and one disillusioned vine leaning on the support. Sometimes an unusual planter starts to set an individual note, but is defeated by its too-familiar contents of snake plant or Swiss cheese plant.

Then again, a planter or combination of planters may contain interesting greenery, but the arrangement does not seem an integral part of the room. Some rooms need a large-scale design of window or wall screening with vines and plants or a floor planter with a tall plant dominating, and this is discussed in Chapter 4. But more often, a smaller design or smaller plants are suitable, with an indoor garden that is planned carefully to be part of the decor of a room.

Sometimes this will mean the accent of a lighted small garden for evening entertaining, planters dramatizing the archway between two rooms, a garden fitted into a room divider. It can be the linking together of windows, by gardens with flowers that follow the color scheme of the room. Vines can be used to emphasize the lines of draperies or a doorway.

In planning indoor gardens that identify closely with their rooms, three ways of approach are suggested. There is the combination of gardens and furniture so that they are literally related. There is the combination of gardens with elements of the room itself. And there are gardens planned to fit the mood of a room in daytime or evening, that can easily be moved.

An example of the first is a coffee table with an inset planter for a garden at center or one end. An inexpensive table that will adapt to having its legs shortened, coffee table height, is easily found with a little shopping around in second-hand stores, or their status-conscious cousins the country antique shops. A square or oblong for the planter is cut out to desired measurements, in the center of a round or square table; either in the center of an oblong table, or at one end if an asymmetric look is wanted. The cutting is done with final proportions in mind, according to the size of the table top, so the planter won't demand too much space or be too near the edge for solid construction.

The work so far can be done by home carpentry. A long-lived planter can be made by a tinsmith, of galvanized metal, to fit in the opening. This should have a narrow right-angled rim. The rim will be supported by quarter round molding, placed to form a ledge on all sides of the open space, slightly below the table top so the rim of the planter will be level with the top of the table. A container can be worked out at home without a tinsmith, using a deep pan, its edges turned back for the rim and soldered as needed at the corners.

This metal planter should be at least five inches deep, to allow for drainage pebbles, soil, and a space above the earth so water and soil won't drift out on the table. If sizable plants are wanted, the planter can be deeper. It should be painted on the outside, for those curious friends who go down on their knees to look under the table and see how the arrangement is contrived.

If the planter is large, depending on the dimensions of the table, two people may be needed to remove it neatly for occasional heavy misting or some rearrangement of the planting. With someone lifting from the bottom, a firm grip can be got by the second person on ends of the planter under the rim, and the moving done without disturbing the plants. For ordinary watering and care, a sheet of plastic can be cut to allow for the planter and protect the table surface.

The plants that will make their home in the coffee table planter will depend on its location. If it is near a window and gets some sunlight, the choice is wider. Also fluorescent lighting can be arranged and a convenient program of lighting worked out. Otherwise, use an arrangement of ferns, and some of the plants mentioned in the chapter on no-sun greenery.

The coffee table with ferns and plants growing out of the table itself makes its own effect, and bric-à-brac on the table should be sparing and carefully chosen. Perhaps a free-form crystal ashtray that adds but does not compete. Perhaps a bowl, picking up the greens of the planter and adding a color that is part of the room's decor.

An attractive unit that blends well into a grouping of chairs and sofa is an end table complete with garden—or a matching set. If space is wanted on the table top for other uses, a small planter can be fitted into it, as with the coffee table. Otherwise the garden takes over all the space, and a different method can be used by getting an unpainted end table, making a wooden planter as described in Chapter 9 that exactly fits the table top, and staining both table and planter the same color. The planter, which rests on the table with no sawed-out hole needed, should of course be caulked so it is watertight, and painted inside with rot resistant. Size here depends on the room and nearby furniture.

When a pair of end tables are used, the planting can match, but more interesting results are gained by using one or two of the same plants in each garden to tie them together, and then deliberately varying the others so there is contrast in foliage and also in height of the plants. If there is space beside an end table, vines can trail down; if a chair is close by, plants are chosen to harmonize; if chair or sofa nearby are patterned or slipcovered in strong colors, then the foliage should be low and compact, with conforming color or merely green leaves.

Furniture that can be adapted for a garden is often found with a little searching in attics and old furniture stores. For example, you may find a chair with simple lines and with broad wooden arms, one of which has an open space with container below for magazines. Then, of course, you make a watertight liner for this container, and have plants growing in the chair arm.

For the second approach, an indoor garden that takes its place as part of the room, or as an indication of two areas of the room, there is the planter combined with a room divider. This has many attractive uses.

Once there were bead curtains, folding screens, sliding doors used liberally to divide sections of a house. Now there is apt to be an open area, wide and well lighted, with a room divider making its indication of living and dining space.

The divider may stand at one side of the entrance to the living room, making a more formalized effect. With a screen of green, it may set apart a special corner for a conversation group of chairs and table.

Depending on the room and its use, plants for the garden in the divider may be low with trailing vines, or higher to add to the screening. As with the coffee table planter, choice of plants depends also on sunlight and other lighting. If color and drama are wanted for some occasion, a potted plant can be sunk in the planter, with its flowers at just the right stage of bloom.

In an apartment, one end of a room can be screened off by garden and divider for a study; for added privacy, a place for quick relaxation, with its comfortable chair, magazine table, and radio; for a cupboard corner, where children can stack their toys and games away in low shelves, and where a few left on the floor won't matter.

Because of the values and attractions of a room divider that is also a garden, and the difficulties of obtaining an attractive one without prohibitive cost, a divider has been worked out for varying uses which is supplied by express. This is shipped with the lumber cut so that it can easily be put together, the planter ready to set in the top, and directions for the simple assembling. The divider is four feet long, a foot wide, and three feet high. Nicholas Orlando, who supplies these (see listing), also supplies custom dividers to specified proportions. The divider is designed with a flat surface at the top beyond the planter, for a choice of purposes.

The divider may be placed with this space of solid top next to the wall, for a tall lamp or vase. Or it may be reversed so that the solid space faces the room and makes a place for a low ornament or low lamp. If the divider separates dining room from kitchen, it can be used with this space next to the wall, for an inconspicuous resting place for salad bowl, toaster, coffee maker. The bottom portion of the divider provides two shelves. These will take books on both sides, making a screen, or may be used for ornaments to give an open effect.

The room divider shown in Figure 4 is the one described above. Here the solid space is next to the wall, as base for a tall vase.

A garden that turns a utility into an attraction uses the top of a radiator placed below a window. This also puts the plants near daylight.

Two things should be considered first, humidity and temperature. A container for water that hooks in back of the radiator should be installed, to improve humidity. Steps should be taken to keep the heat from the plants; of several methods for this, two of the easiest are to have a sheet of asbestos cut the right size to fit the radiator top with a slight overhang, or to make a thick pad of newspapers covered with material of a color that suits the room, perhaps the color of radiator or window frame.

The planter for the garden is of wood or metal, with measurements according to the size of the radiator top. If a simpler process is wanted, get two or three of the narrow window boxes sold by hardware stores, the number depending on the length of the radiator, and use these along the front. Behind them, on pans of pebbles, place a row of plants in pots, these pots mainly concealed by the window boxes. Water in the pans, kept lower than the bottom of the pots, provides further humidity. In the window boxes can be arrangements of small plants purchased at a nursery, plants grown from seeds, ferns or vines. If you get and plant an extra window box, this can stay in a specially sunny window, where seedlings thrive and flowers bloom, and then this window box can be exchanged for one of the others in rotation. If wide pots are used, an insulated shelf should be built out beyond the radiator, or the window boxes be allowed to extend out a little with asbestos or newspaper pad at the front.

Among the types of gardens that seem part of the architectural design of a room, a built-in bookcase adapts easily. Fluorescent tubes for use with plants, such as Sylvania Gro-Lux, are installed on the bottom of a shelf, and the space below the lights is fitted with a planter, of metal or wood, slightly less wide than the shelf so it can be readily removed and replaced. As with all wooden planters, if wood is chosen, it should be tested after waterproofing to make sure all cracks are caulked before soil is put in. A heavy plastic sheet, cut to size, may be used for a lining of the planter, if there is concern about damp and books on a shelf below. The metal planter saves these steps but adds a trip to the tinsmith.

Here is a good place to experiment with different flowering plants, to find out their response to light. While the experimenting is going on, miniature begonias make a steady basis for the planting design. A variety of begonias gives choice of interesting foliage as well as the promise of flowers. Suggestions for this garden are found in Chapter 15.

This lighted garden repays a careful plan of arrangement. A design suggested in one of the chapters, or your own garden plan, will build toward a unified effect without a look of haphazard scattering or bunching of plants.

A do-it-yourself project that dramatizes vines is the addition of a circular garden to a pole lamp. This container should be of metal, clamped tightly in place. To make less weight, small plants should be chosen that don't need deep earth, and vines featured. If you use a deep round pan with a hole cut in the middle for the pole, after supporting it with a clamped collar and angled metal strips, caulk it thoroughly around the joining of pole and container. You could use an angel-food cake pan fitted to the pole with a spacer made of rubber, and screwed to the pole. If preferred, a plant pole can be purchased, with planting space provided. Train the vines up the pole toward the lights with loops of thin wire twisted to the pole as you would fasten a plant tie to a stake. If you leave the lights on generously, vines will be interested in their own climbing.

Rooms with the fireplace in an unfortunate position because of the chimney's location, or a fireplace with uninspired lines, can gain interest from mantel gardens. This garden can stay in place much of the year, but be moved as wished when the fire is lighted.

Here the emphasis should be on foliage plants that rise in attractive patterns, and vines that trail lushly down. Usually no-sun plants are the easiest to manage, though some mantels get a sweep of sunlight.

An assist in training vines is useful, so that they make a pattern or wander with seeming negligence exactly where you want them. Take one of the green bamboo stakes bought at hardware stores for garden use, a slender one, and cut it into different lengths, some as short as three inches. These tiny stakes, slanted into the earth at the correct angle, will bend a vine lower, or direct its trailing course. Two stakes together, crossed at the top, will keep a vine in position till it has settled there. The green of the stakes makes them unobtrusive.

Since the planter itself will be much in evidence in its high position, a good choice is one of the oblong, deep ceramic containers with simple lines, stocked by many garden shops. Or if a waterproof box is made to fit the space, although staining is usually preferable to painting, here an exception could be made and the box painted to match the mantel.

The third category—gardens that fit a room and its mood, and may easily be moved from one place to another—is pleasantly flexible. Thus a garden may be planted for a given room, with flowers that enhance this room but can't live permanently in its lack of sunlight. They can stay most of the time comfortably in their movable planter in a sunny window, and shift to their special room on important occasions.

Planters may be planned that suit more than one room, according to the time and the use. This involves careful choices in container and contents, but is convenient.

A variation of this movable planter is one with subdued lighting of its own. This is illustrated in Figure 5. It can be plugged in at an outlet in the front hall when guests are expected, to make an effective welcome. On another occasion, it will light the table softly where preparations for a buffet supper are waiting for the proper moment in the evening. It can brighten a dull corner on a dark afternoon. The contents of this planter are chosen according to the rooms where it will be used, with perhaps only white flowers, or a color that will harmonize, or only green plants and vines.

The planter shown was designed for me by my husband, to be used in an archway between two rooms. It has opaque glass panels, so a soft light is thrown up against the foliage. It was done in copper, which polishes to a rosy sheen, but a darker color may be preferred. Its dimensions are eighteen by fourteen, with a depth of four and a half inches. One side has been made wider to allow for the electric fittings; the opposite side can be made to match, with more total width or with a small loss in planting space.

If this planter is made by a tinsmith, he will only need the dimensions desired and an explanation of how the space is divided. This division is simple. An oblong container is made, with a broad rim. This box is divided by partitions into four spaces. The space along one side, two and a quarter inches wide at the top, is sealed off after the electric fittings are in place, with the cord coming out a small hole at the back of the planter, and sockets fitted into holes at each end. Along the two ends of the planter are compartmented spaces, two and a half inches wide at the top, where the light bulbs will be, with the top of the partitions bent into a tiny L-shaped

Figure 5

Ted Budlong

The photograph above shows the planter lighted. Its contents are described in this chapter. The lower photograph shows the interior, with the arrangement for light bulbs and glass panels.

rim to support the glass, and two metal lips soldered on the box side for the opposite supports. The remaining largest space, of course, is for the plants. The second photograph shows the empty planter with glass panels removed, so details can be seen.

The planter slants in toward the bottom to give better lines. The tinsmith can get the electric wire with plug, and the two sockets to which it is to be connected, or you can supply them. Nothing more is needed to complete the planter except two panels of opaque glass, cut to fit the top of the end compartments, and two long 15-watt opaque bulbs.

The planter can be altered, with wider or narrower rim or a different slope for the sides, but it should not be more shallow. It is watertight, soldered at all necessary points, without drainage holes, so depth is needed for drainage pebbles.

As illustrated, it is planted with trailing ivy that extends over the light panels for a leaf shadow effect; a miniature palm, which takes the light interestingly; a heath *Erica carnea* 'Winter Beauty,' which sprays out at the front left; and the lower small rhododendron at the front right. The plants are arranged so that there is a swirl that reaches its high point at the back left corner, and reaches its lowest point diagonally across the planter at the front right. At the center is a low clump of dwarf marigolds, lemon yellow, that adds a color but does not detract from the swirl of foliage.

If you know someone who enjoys shop work, and turns out anything from bird feeders to sets of shelves, ask him to make you a bookends garden. All that is needed is a broad board for base, two uprights at each end, spaced to allow half a dozen books between, and in the center a long narrow box for the garden. This box can be a deep pan, set inside a wooden frame, which will simplify providing a watertight container that won't start a small brook running toward the books. And as said before, choice of plants will depend on the amount of daylight that will reach the planter. You can use no-sun foliage plants, or bring in small pots with well-sunned contents, to be sunk into the soil for a visit.

A desk planter, centered under a fluorescent light, is a place for African violets or some of the other gesneriads. This can be one of the deep ceramic planters carried by garden shops.

If you don't have a fluorescent light, ordinary incandescent bulbs encourage some plants. A garden can be combined with a standard lamp that has its wire either emerging high on the base, or well insulated from contact with water. The lamp can stand in one corner of a box planter, with long trails of ivy trained around its base, so the planter and light are caught together by green leaves.

Since this third category of gardens permits a wide selection of plants in rooms with little sunlight, by rotating them from sunny locations, study your apartment or house, measuring sunlight, to find the best window to use as a sun base. There a wide shelf can be prepared, or if space is limited, the back of a table or desk can be cleared for sunning planters.

Small planters, like those described in Chapter 6, of course are simple to manage. But if a larger garden is wanted, for interest in a sunless room, this also can be easily managed. My rock garden pictured in Figure 12 is placed on an old piano bench fitted with casters, to be rolled back and forth from morning sunlight to afternoon shade in another room.

A way to vary small planters in combination with each other is to place them on the shelves of a cake stand. Each planter contains a miniature garden or arrangement. These can be dotted about the house in the sun and, as the plants bud and flower, moved to the stand. One of the planters should hold vines, so there is a green tracery between the shelves.

While considering equipment for hospitality that can be adapted to gardens, a tea cart can switch to a garden cocktail bar. An oblong planter stretches across an end, next to the handle by which the cart is pushed. Ferns and tall plants make a background for the tray of glasses and bottles and ice.

If these two are too conversation-piece, and something modern in effect is wanted for a room, try plants in an arrangement of glass blocks that have an open side and plenty of space inside, fitting the cool straight lines of the blocks together in a design.

The main consideration—whether garden and furniture are

combined, garden and some feature of the room worked out
together, or gardens planned to be moved about to fit the
needs of a room—is to relate the garden to the room's decor.
The word "decor" has been taken over to mean the decorative
scheme; more strictly it derives from the Latin word that
translates "to be suitable." A carefully planned garden can illustrate both meanings.

Changing a room by fresh paint, new curtains, added furniture works out best, of course, when the changes are part of
a detailed plan to gain a specific quality. This may be bright-
ness in a dark house, coolness in warm climates, restfulness,
an impact of individual color combination and line. It may
go further, with expertise, to achieve a more intricate effect.
In the same way, the indoor garden is planned to fit the key-
note of the room, to harmonize with the main effect, and only
then does it make its own claim of interest.

An exception to this generality is when the garden is used
permanently or temporarily as a conversation piece. Even then,
dramatic as the whole arrangement may be with lights and
color, the planter should have a relation to the room, so a very
modern planter isn't used in a room with period furniture, or
a garden contrived in an old-fashioned desk with carved wood-
work isn't set down in a streamlined room.

The wrong combinations are obvious, the right ones fun to
plan and satisfying to work out. The choice of whether to
make an important change by a room divider with its own
garden, or dramatize a sideboard with the lighted planter, or
group chairs around the coffee table with its ferns growing
gracefully from the center, will hinge on the room and what
you want to do with it.

Then when the basic arrangement is decided, added effect
is gained from the contents of the planter. Whether they are
foliage plants, vines, flowers or a combination, they will
achieve more when they are planted to form a garden, with
composition and character.

This goes a long way beyond the simple matter of growing
plants in the house. This means an indoor garden that has its
individual character, but that also blends with the room's
decor.

4. Larger Gardens

A RELATIVELY LARGE GARDEN WITH TALL PLANTS OR LONG VINES can often solve a special problem in apartment or house. It can screen a window which looks out on a bleak neighboring building; change a dull corner to a dramatic composition of lighted foliage; turn a blank stretch of room wall into a trellis with vines.

Also it can give depth to a small room, with a tiered planting against a background of higher foliage. In a room with a badly placed door or window, the garden can shift emphasis and provide a better balance. A box-shaped entrance hall changes its character with a high shelf of plants and a light behind them. A room that needs brightening gains a lift from hanging baskets of flowering vine, two or three of them at different levels, near enough together so they complement each other and seem an airy garden swinging lightly.

When there is no problem, the large indoor garden is still an effective addition to a room. One of the possibilities is a floor planter.

The floor planter may feature one large plant of interesting shape, as shown in Figure 6, with the other plants lower. Two large plants may be used, or any grouping that combines well and suits the room.

The planter itself must have depth for root space for a large plant. Though some floor planters have drainage holes and an outsized saucer, the effect is of an overgrown pot and the line is lost. But a preferable planter, without drainage holes, must be tall enough to allow for a deep layer of pebbles and charcoal.

If there is time in the program to make and take care of a floor planter that stretches across one corner of a room, this is a project with many possible variations. For this, a triangular planter can be made of galvanized metal, its size depending on how far the garden can extend out from the corner.

The rim of the planter must be high enough to allow for a space above the soil to simplify watering. A felt pad between floor and planter prevents possible scratches on the floor boards.

This corner garden should achieve height, and the total effect should be of definite shape and strong detail, rather than of delicacy. Selection of plants again starts with the question of lighting. The chosen corner may have sunlight part of the day, which simplifies the matter. It may have its own special lights, which would influence a choice. Or if not well lighted, there is a more limited but satisfactory group of plants, as discussed in Chapter 10.

Some large plants should be acquired at once, rather than buying all small ones for later growth. Information from the supplier will give the needs of the plants you like, as to light required, and you can fit your final choice to the lighting of your chosen corner.

As much as possible, the plants should prefer the same type of soil, but exceptions can have their underground compartmenting. Plants requiring a great deal of humidity should be avoided, though grouping of plants together helps this aspect a bit, and spraying as indicated will also help.

Among the possibilities for this floor planter is Chinese evergreen, which likes shade and grows strongly. Dracaena

Figure 6

Ted Budlong

Dracaena marginata, *rising tall with its three rosettes of pointed leaves, is featured in the floor planter. Lower plants are a bromeliad and a gesneriad, described later, at the right, with* Hoya 'Hindu Rope' *trailing over the edge at the left.*

plants offer a variety of bright foliage, which holds its color
better if it has good light in winter months (Figure 10).
Monstera deliciosa, which has two menu-like popular names,
Mexican breadfruit and Swiss cheese plant, though unin-
teresting in a pot alone, combines well here, adding a broad
spread of perforated leaves to the design. A tall fiddle-leaf
fig will supply sizable leaves, without indentations.

This wide planter is the place for a bark-covered post to
support vines or, better, an interestingly shaped forked branch.
It should be based firmly against a wall of the planter, usually
a back wall, with a support such as bricks which will be
covered later with soil, or a rock pile that can emerge above
the earth. For an accent among the solid greens of other vines,
ivy-arum has definitely spotted leaves.

Toward the front, lower plants add to the pattern. Whether
they have strongly marked foliage, sharply pointed leaves, or a
heavily massed expanse of green is a matter of relationship to
the whole arrangement you are building. If there is sufficient
humidity in the room, you could add a peperomia you like for
its well-marked leaves. A fern with definite fronds, such as
the holly or Boston fern, will break the front rim of the
planter. Ivy can be trained along the rim, with small sections
of green bamboo stakes restraining it from wandering too far
beyond the planter.

To return to possible problems, a window screen of vines
and plants will compensate for a poor view outside, while
giving the plants daylight. There are plenty of plants that will
accept a sunless window. With sun, you can think in wider
terms of flowers, of course, as well as foliage.

An easily made basis for your leafy screen is a series of glass
shelves, set on brackets, running across the window at different
points. They may be the same distance apart. But with a little
more time allowed for plant searching, a good effect is made
by having the shelves farther apart toward the bottom for
taller plants, graduating up with nearer shelves for small
plants. The number of shelves is affected by whether you are
working toward a simple effect stressing vines, or a more
complex design that will need more shelves.

The use of glass permits light to filter through between containers, lets attention center on the plants, relates to the window panes at the back, and gives an airy feel to the whole. The shelves are cut to measurements in a few minutes at the glazier's or hardware store; the brackets, with their lip to hold the glass, and long screws are all else that's needed for the shelves.

As you begin to collect interesting plants for these shelves, it may be a temptation to leave them in their plastic or clay pots, which is fatal for an effective screen. Each shelf should have its main planter, long and narrow, preferably one of the severe-lined ceramic planters with matching saucer sold at garden shops. These are set in different positions on the shelves, to vary emphasis and make a linked pattern, which can be asymmetric, balanced, or wander curving from the large planter at the lower left up across the shelves to the dominating planter on the higher right.

Arranged at the sides of these main planters are the small containers. These should be planned with a definite color scheme in mind, and with the colors keyed low so containers won't be more demanding of attention than their contents. They can be as varied in size and shape as suits the overall pattern, and a great deal of time can happily be spent setting the small containers in one place and another along the shelves, and stepping back six paces to view the result.

Try to transplant to planters and small containers a day or so before the plants move to the window. In the meantime, keep them in shade, sufficiently well watered.

Vines are an important part of the window screen, trailing down between the shelves, making a leaf pattern. Use vines that will grow with enthusiasm, such as the philodendrons, for early effect, and add more varied ones as you go. You will need to control the direction of the vines, spreading them, turning them in different directions, and a discreet use of Scotch tape is an aid, folded at the center so it doesn't cling to or bind the vine, spreading at each end for attaching.

In general, ornaments are out of place on the shelves, and tend to give a fussy appearance. But a single one on a central shelf, for focus, can be effective. For example, a crystal bird.

Another exception to the use of bric-à-brac on the shelves among the planters and containers is to use glass of a single category, so there is a unifying effect. A successful window screen was made by combining a collection of miniature glass pitchers and African violets. Using only African violets unified the effect, and provided their own colors. The pitchers harmonized with glass shelves and window panes, and had their uniform shape, with soft colors of pale green, light blue, and amber. The shelves for this screen were set rather close, and no vines were used. Sunlight slanting through the flowers and glass pitchers brought out a changing pattern.

Another treatment of a window is with hanging baskets. They can be in front of the window, at each side in balance, or when the window is near a room corner, they can be suspended on long brackets attached to the nearby right-angled wall.

Containers are of early importance here. Shopping around in florist stores, garden centers, the garden section of department stores, will give an idea of the possibilities. Of course you want a non-dripping hanging basket; this need has been met by containers on chains, with a saucer attached at the bottom. Fine, functionally, but the saucer may make you feel as though a table had just been removed from beneath, and the total effect is uninspired. A better selection is a well-shaped hanging container, often bowl-shaped or square, that has a second container inside. This liner container can be taken out as needed. It will have drainage holes, so water will run into the outside container. There should be a space for this at the bottom, and if the inside container isn't fitted high enough, pebbles can be used under it.

The hanging baskets can each be planted differently, a low one with a carefully laid-out garden of small plants, a higher one with taller plants and vines, one at the top all vines. Or a single basket can be used, its contents related to its height, the window, the room. All of these hanging containers are likely to be called baskets, though you won't use mesh or a basket of wire and moss without some provision underneath for dripping water.

Hanging baskets may be suspended from a ceiling hook or swung on brackets. If your hanging garden is high enough, a double-container combination can be dispensed with. The single container can have an ordinary flowerpot set in it on pebbles, a low enough pot to be out of sight. This flowerpot can be used for an arrangement of plants, or a single dramatic one. Or again, you may find a redwood basket that you can fit with an inner container, or a shallow swinging white bowl, in which may be set a low white pot of flowers.

For a single effect in a high basket, there is lipstick plant, and also coral plant. Both have attractive red flowers, those of the lipstick plant more orange, when hung in sunlight. *Hypocyrta wettsteinii* is a graceful plant for a hanging basket (Figure 17).

Among the many begonias, one can be found for the light of a given window, full sun or simple daylight. Begonias have attractive foliage as well as flowers, and are sturdy growers. They are a good starting plant, while you search further or experiment.

Since *Hedera helix* or English ivy is available in many varieties, a choice is easy for size or shape of leaves to fit a design. This should have sun and frequent spraying. Creeping fig will trail or climb. For a window without sun, Kenilworth ivy—*Cymbalaria muralis*—is attractive and grows well.

In one sunny window can be an experimental garden, in a good-sized planter at windowsill level, fitted with bamboo poles. Here you can plant your own seeds, for your own vines. Try maurandia vine, which will grow and flower in the winter. The cup-and-saucer vine, *Cobaea scandens,* can be grown from seed. Or grow one of the vines you like in your outside garden. If short stakes or poles are used at first, and taller ones added as the vines grow, there won't be a waiting period with an array of high empty stakes.

A trellis is effective against a room wall, or between two areas. This can be started from the floor with a low planter, or from a planter on a table, or from the room divider.

A lattice can be made of wooden strips. Also a wide-meshed wire screen can be fastened to a frame. This is secured firmly to the planter, which should be large enough so it makes a substantial base.

There can be a flower garden with vines rising from it. Or ground cover and low plants can be used to make a mass of green, with the vines taking all the emphasis.

The trellis, dark green, will make enough support for most vines. But you may want to wind them in and out in a good line, or secure them with loops of green garden twine, in correct position. A wall trellis which will be misted needs simple protection for the wall behind it. The wall should be protected by a coat of good grade marine varnish, which is clear and will let the color of the wall show through.

When used against a wall, rather than as a screening divider, the lattice can be more narrow, or taper in regular steps toward the top. All of this is affected by the space to be covered and the final effect wanted. A small screening arrangement can be made with bamboo poles and wire strung between them, but this is apt to sag and lose its pattern.

Vines can be shopped for, chosen from suggestions here, brought back from previous experience and memories. And one of the climbing philodendrons can well be included; they may seem ubiquitous, but they are adaptable to different conditions of light, heat, and humidity, and they grow vigorously. One indoor arrangement of philodendron, rising from a single large pot, wandered up the wall and across much of the ceiling of a sizable room, assisted discreetly by wires, but always spreading on.

A garden stretching across under two windows that have a space of wall between them gives new interest to that side of the room. The planter should end level with the outside of the window frames. It can be on strong supporting brackets, or its own wooden legs, according to the versatility of home carpentry.

Here with a long space to make use of, contrast can be worked out in the height of plants, perhaps taller in the center against the wall, or taller at one end of the planter with foliage in front of that window. The whole space is one garden, and should be planned accordingly, for appearance. The plan should make provision for the middle section, with plants that will do well without much direct sunlight. If you decide on height at one end of the garden, you could start an ivy tree, training it on a shape of twisted wire. This is a project interesting in its slow development, as well as when completed.

A zebra plant, one of the bromeliads, with its barred leaves (Figure 8) goes effectively in this garden, planted on higher ground where it doesn't get too much water. Some of the dracaenas should be considered, for their decorative foliage and amenability to house conditions. With the space and room firmly in mind, a series of visits to nurseries will provide appropriate plants and may trigger a new idea for the whole design.

Vine screens, hanging gardens, floor planters or glass-shelved window gardens, wall trellises—these larger garden arrangements can make an important addition to a room. They may solve a problem, as suggested. In addition, they are pleasant gardens to live with.

5. *Nostalgia Gardens*

THERE IS MUCH MOVING ABOUT THE COUNTRY NOWADAYS, FOR business reasons, for health or an adventurous interest in new places, or toward the greener grass on the other side of the country. Families find new friends and schools and interests. But sometimes, when one is contentedly settled in a new part of the country, there can be moments of remembering an earlier home with nostalgia. It may be for woods or plains or sea or hills that have been left behind. And we say, "I wish I had a photograph of that," meaning something more than a special scene or hill—a quality remembered.

For these times, and to keep a small piece of that familiar countryside close at hand, a miniature garden can be better than a photograph. It has the scent and feel as well as the look, a living scene.

A nostalgia garden answers that glance back over the shoulder toward earlier home country. It also gives friends in the new locality an introduction to that country.

An indoor garden can be detailed to copy a specific place, and this is discussed in another chapter. The nostalgia garden, however, is more general, and intended to give the feel and characteristic quality of some part of the country. It is best as a wildlife garden, reflecting your memories of walks and views from a hill and long looks from a car window.

You may be wanting a garden that features cactus and open stretches; a seaside view with dune grass—white sand—low shrubs, with a curving bay shore that slopes down to water; steep rocky inclines with footholds for vines; tropical foliage with bright splashes of red and yellow. Whatever part of the country you choose to represent, appropriate plants and supplies may be ordered for it. But there can be a more personal source than commercial suppliers, if friends and relatives ship what you need.

Also you may want to take plants and adjuncts with you, when you return from a visit to your former home. This can be done with many plants, if you work carefully. Take the ones you particularly like, and a good percentage of them will travel and adjust to their new environment. You might make notes of their growing conditions; how damp, how much shade. Have solid containers for the trip, which can be metal or plastic boxes fitted with a carrying handle, or deep pans if you are driving. A small watering pot will save time en route.

Frequent checking for dampness is half the battle, while traveling. A one-inch fragile fern growing on a chip of bark traveled well with me during a week of summer motoring, bedded in moss that held moisture.

Be sure to check if you are free from any local laws restricting transport of plants across a state line. While you are selecting plants, and before you start to dig, note whether the plants are likely to stay reasonably small, so you won't be misled by a young plant with its two-foot relatives far in the background.

If you have transplanted wild flowers and plants before, you will know to take a good quantity of earth around the roots, loosening it as little as possible. This ball of earth should be secured with a piece of sacking or plastic. If plastic is used, there should be small holes made at the bottom. A good method of closing the top bag-wise is to use the plastic covered wires, twist-ties, sold in garden shops. These can be thrust through the cloth or plastic at intervals to prevent slipping and can be opened easily to check for proper moisture. Don't fasten them too tightly around the stems of the plants; put a collar in between of damp sphagnum moss, or if you don't have that, of damp tissue paper, to offset bruising of the stems. Plants can also be put in clay pots, and set in damp moss in the container for the trip.

If you are driving and have space, take an extra box or tight bag of earth, from the locality where you got your plants, to provide at-home soil for your garden. If this is impossible, at least make a general check of the soil where the plants are growing: for example, it may be sandy and the plants will need less moisture; it may be woods soil with much leaf mold and tend to be acid; it may contain organic matter and retain moisture. Your nurseryman can advise on soil approximating natural conditions. And you will have as a sample of earth in the ball around roots of the plants.

The planter you use for this garden can be a window box, a really deep pottery container. But you will have more space for an interesting scene if you waterproof a square or oblong box about six inches deep and at least a foot wide, preferably wider. This can be open to the air, just the box with leaves and vines curving over the edges, or it can be glassed-in as described in Chapter 9. The choice will depend on the type of plants you are going to have, the amount of humidity needed.

An example of a nostalgia garden, ready to bring back half-caught memories, is one that is characteristic of the northern woods. Anyone questioning the combination of woods and garden need only think of a woodland carpeting of violets, bluebells under trees, anemones or ladyslippers beyond a slanting branch, arbutus among fallen leaves.

It is true, however, that this garden should be natural looking, without balancing of plants or formal effects. There can be a clearing in the midst of trees and bushes, a thicket in one corner, even a path that wanders unevenly as an animal might make a trail to water, but it should all be as you would find the real woods, done small-scale.

Woodland must have trees, of course, and if possible real ones. Miniature trees belong here, some larger than those chosen for a rock garden, some relatively smaller to group with bushes. If the house is kept too warm for these, select plants that can be trimmed to arch out at the top, giving an effect of branches. But quite a few miniature evergreens tolerate indoor living when well watered and occasionally misted.

With some form of foliage, then, work out a leafy or needled lacework overhead, so light will fall patterned, as in larger woods, through the canopy of branches. Some well-shaped smaller trees can be saved to use near the front.

All across the back of the planter will be thick little bushes, so the woods will seem to extend back indefinitely. These bushes should continue at the sides of the planter, at least half-way to the front.

Are you going to have a closely planted little woods, heavy with underbrush? Or are you leaving an open glade, for flowers or special details? The plan should be worked out on paper and marked off into halves and quarters, because it is easy to get interested in the planting and find suddenly you have used up half the glade space with bushes.

A design that takes a little longer, but is worth the time, is one that provides a special vista through trees and bushes. It will be partly concealed, till the observer moves to one side, gets the right angle—then there is a clear view between trees and bushes to reveal a clump of crimson-tipped lichen against a tiny log, a hidden pool, or clusters of bright berries near white birch bark.

Planting time starts as usual with a drainage layer of pebbles and charcoal at the bottom, and soil built up from a minimum of two inches to higher mounds and slopes. For this garden, the soil should be rich in humus. If you don't have a woods available from which to get soil dark with leaf mold, humus can be obtained from a nursery or garden center. Many of the plants and trees will prefer an acid soil, and for others you can use the insulating barriers of slate and foil. If you transported the plants yourself, you may have brought extra soil from the original site, and anyway will have largish balls of earth around the roots. Spaces dug in the planter will be wide, to allow for the native soil.

Set together for special placement any plants needing more sunlight than the others, so they can be put in an open space, or near the sides, where sunlight comes between bushes. This can be noted on the plan.

Also put in one place everything needed to make the vista through the woods: sufficient shrubbery and the details of the hidden scene. A vista of this sort will be more successful if it is thoroughly worked out in advance.

Some of the plants and trees, whether found or bought, can thrive in either an open planter or a terrarium. But in choosing others, a decision has to be made as to which type of container will be used.

With a terrarium, you will lose the miniature evergreens, but tall branching ferns can be substituted, which at least will make a roof of fronds. You will gain the possibility of a marshy corner, where the woods slopes down to a hollow, perhaps with tiny stepping stones across. Here where a section is walled off underground, and the soil stays especially damp with perhaps some sphagnum moss added, can be a place for small northern pitcher plants, and a clump of venus's-flytrap, or venus flytrap as it is commonly called, with its fringed and hinged leaves ready to trap insects.

A small rock fern that does well in a terrarium is ebony spleenwort. Goldthread is a good plant here. Pipsissewa can be used under glass or in the open.

Ferns can be used lavishly in a terrarium, without the chore of frequent checking to make sure that earth is damp enough. Several small ferns set together make a good effect, as well as illustrating a remembered spot in real woods where the ferns grew thickly. Among the ferns to consider are *Pteris ensiformis evergemiensis*, *Polystichum tsus-simense*, and maidenhair. Wild ferns will grow tall for the arching roof, and can be cut back as a frond grows out of proportion.

The use of an open planter is worth the extra time in watering, when possible in the program, for this particular garden. Choosing of small evergreen trees is a pleasure in itself. Walter Kolaga of Mayfair Nurseries (see listing) has a variety of miniature trees for shipping, which should do well indoors with proper culture. Among his many small trees are *Chamaecyparis lawsoniana forsteckiana* and *Chamaecyparis obtusa nana*, both cypress; a column-shaped juniper, *Juniperus communis compressa*; a slow-growing Japanese yew, *Taxus cuspidata minima*; and an arborvitae, *Thuja occidentalis ohlendorffii*.

You may prefer a more open woods, without a roofing of branches, that shows details more readily. But if you want a branched effect overhead, one way to achieve this is to select carefully three or four dwarf trees, larger than the miniatures, with reaching branches, and space them about the planter so their branches meet. You may need to do some strategic pruning to get the right effect. These larger trees should be planted first, with their roots spread comfortably across the bottom of the planter; then soil added, and perhaps rocks set about temporarily to prop a tree correctly or mark where its roots are, until the rest of the planting is done.

The choice of plants may depend on the particular stretch of woods that is being recalled, or may be a general illustration of northern woodland. You could remember gathering wintergreen, or perhaps you called it checkerberry. Wild strawberry plants have attractive leaves, all apart from their flowers and berries. The open planter also may have a lower corner, where you can put plants that like damper soil, among them tufts of cranberry, which will lift in sprays of small leaves as well as creep.

As you gather plants, some of them can be used to make a small garden for a centerpiece. A glass or china bowl makes a good container, deep enough to take pebbles and soil (Figure 7).

Some of the plants and flowers offered by Arthur Eames Allgrove will recall early walks in the woods. There is trailing arbutus—and how often have we heard someone say that arbutus hasn't been seen for years. Picnicking parties have torn out much arbutus, but it still can grow in your garden. There is creeping snowberry, partridge-berry, bearberry. Myrtle

Figure 7

Ira Finke

Small plants make a centerpiece garden, in a crystal dessert dish.
Peperomia capreata 'Emerald Ripple' *is at the center, and around it are*
woods plants such as pipsissewa, goldthread, club moss, and a walking
fern.

trails and lifts and trails again, giving an undergrowth effect
in your small woods.

In order to include some plants you want especially, you
should note their preferences and habits in some detail.
Arbutus, for example, could be planted in its own pot, sunk
and concealed, since to bloom in the spring it needs a dormant
period, and can be removed then and replaced with something
else. When plants are purchased you can check for details of
their culture.

When you gather your own, your memories and detective
work help. If you want to try some particular things because
of their associations, that is part of the pleasure of this garden.
You may want a piece of Virginia creeper, a small huckleberry
bush, a special creeping plant you used to gather. Never mind
if you are told these will never live indoors. Every so often
this warning will not hold true, and you'll have the personal
achievement of showing some wild violet that was not sup-
posed to live a month inside a house now growing well half

a year later, or a plant usually tagged "outdoors only" which you have provided with homelike conditions and which has settled in to stay.

There is a warning encountered occasionally about lady-slippers, the wild orchids you will remember nodding gracefully under the trees. It is said sometimes that these will not transplant and live many years. However, this has been disproved. Yellow ladyslipper is transplanted for a contented life of over a dozen years, and pink ladyslipper, more difficult in culture, has been reported for ten years of transplanted life.

You might try your hand at growing yellow ladyslippers indoors. If you are using an open planter, put one ladyslipper there, and a second under glass in its own small container. Ground limestone should be added in the soil around the lady-slippers, if your soil is acid, to tone it down.

Thickets are part of a woods scene, and for the miniature woods many plants that are creepers and ground cover in ordinary life take on a higher stature, in the small-scale setting. The thickets should have varying height.

Pixie moss is remembered by many people who searched for the small white flowers in spring, half hidden under brown leaves. This can be ordered in pots, to be set out to spread. There is also miterwort. If there is no red showing on your partridge-berry, it still remains an excellent thicket.

If you have a problem corner, a back edge of the planter to be concealed, a need for bush effects somewhere, and don't have appropriate plants for this, there is something which may not have the right associations but gives a good small-leaved effect. This is boxwood, which as you know can be pruned rigorously, and so shaped to your needs. Look for *Boxus microphylla japonica*, or inquire for a slow-growing, small-leaved box.

Everywhere in the woods moss will be needed. Not only for ground cover, but for an impression of cool green hollows and smooth mounds. Varieties of moss are listed in catalogs, but when you collect your own, you put a personal stamp on the scene. When walking in the woods, look along the crevices of exposed tree roots, on fallen logs, in shaded places, and on the banks of streams, where you may find a tree fallen and lying half in the water, with moss spreading along it. Some mosses will take dryer conditions, and keep these separate for use on higher ground.

With moss, as with the plants you gather, of course, firm the ground where you have removed something, so neighboring growth won't be disrupted. Don't take all of a group of plants, but leave some to renew and spread. Remember the vanishing arbutus, and take a plant here, a plant there, with care for the plants and earth you leave.

If you are exploring in new territory, and the woods is near a house, an inquiry will make sure you are free to take some small specimens. This not only is correct procedure, but often results in interested cooperation as to where plants may be found.

While in the woods or country, keep watch for unusual pieces of bark, particularly with lichen on them. A fallen branch may have an interesting twist or knot, and a piece can be broken off to include it. Where there are birches, there is apt to be a curl of bark on the ground nearby. These and similar small things will add a lot later when details are wanted. Perhaps there are tiny cones, perhaps acorns on the ground. If you come across a large acorn cup, save it for a container for its own bit of earth and moss.

Also keep a lookout for a piece of rock that has a hollow in it deep enough for planting. There may also be a small rock with lichen.

For those who are not visiting northern woods, a supplier who has many familiar wild flowers and plants for shipping is Thomas M. Wood (see listing). Mr. Wood has wild plants growing profusely in a half-acre of land fenced against deer, since the deer enjoyed eating arbutus and trillium. A slat roof of shade-strips, lying north and south, gives his ferns and plants just enough sunlight.

He not only has goldthread, miterwort, partridge-berry, ebony spleenwort fern, hairy lip fern, and mountain shield fern, for regular indoor use, but his catalog lists many other wild flowers and plants and you may want to try some of these and see if you can reproduce a home setting so comfortable they accept indoor life. The catalog gives suggestions for culture.

When the planter is partially landscaped, with taller trees planted if these are used, with bushes at the rear and the back portions of the sides, the rest depends on the design that has been worked out and noted down on paper. Choice of a tangle of thickets, a group of miniature trees, an open glade, will determine much of the space.

Before the main part is planted, though, the outline of the vista should be marked out on the earth with pebbles or toothpicks. First locate where the concealed scene will be, toward one side and no further front than midpoint. Allow enough space for it. Then mark out positions for foliage plants and clumps of fern or trees, which will mainly conceal the scene.

To illustrate, suppose the scene that is deep in the woods consists of clumps of lichen, lifting from the ground like incredibly small flowers—pixie caps, rising perhaps an inch high, or the lichen called British soldier, with its bright red tips. A slanting miniature log lies just beyond them, accenting them.

Directly in front of this scene, and turning in an ell at the right side, are shielding bushes, so only a glimpse may be caught of something interesting there beyond the leaves. Then place two plants slanting away from the scene in a screen at the left, leave a space, and set out three plants in a second screen in front, so you have an effect like high hedges on two sides of a road, that leads from the scene toward the left corner of the box. Standing directly in front of the planter, you see only the screening bushes, in front of the scene and then angling toward the front. Move to the left, and a space opens up, like an alley slanting in. There at the end of the open long space, down which you are looking, you can see the bright lichen against the log. The scene and the slant of the vista can be varied indefinitely, in any arrangement that shields a special grouping of interest and color and permits it to be seen unexpectedly from only one direction.

In making the general plan, remember to allow the unshaded spot of plants that need more sun. If you are using a lot of high branches and tall foliage plants, and have one plant you want to feature that requires more sunlight than it's likely to get, sink it pot and all in the ground, and take it out periodically for a week of sunning. This won't work for everything, but is worth trying, and your plant may decide to compromise.

Whatever detail work you have chosen, you will have at the end a miniature stretch of woodland, with plants reminiscent of the actual northern woods. Some plants may be chosen for this reminiscent value, others for the general effect. There will be moss and tiny vines, perhaps a seedling from a full-sized tree, bits of pine needle and fragments of bark on the ground, with the foliage shadows swaying across them.

Looking into this nostalgia garden, catching the scent of moss and evergreen and cool earth, you recapture something of faraway tall woods. A breeze comes through the window, or air stirs from an opened door, so the leaves and needles move softly together, alive there in your woods.

6. Movable Gardens

SMALL GARDENS THAT CAN EASILY BE MOVED FROM ONE PLACE TO
another are used as carefully planned accents for a room, as
a centerpiece for the dining table, as a means of bringing new
interest to the living room when different gardens are used on
different days. These planters take care of easy rotation. When
the colors of containers and flowers are planned suitably, one
garden may fit into place in two or three rooms. If there is a
difficulty with color schemes, a planter of a muted color with
all green foliage is adaptable.

Some versions of these planters have been called dish gardens. There are two bad connotations for this name: the frequent use of containers that are too shallow and without
drainage holes, and the tendency of some commercial dish
gardens to contain plants needing different types of care that
often grow to disproportionate heights. However, small gardens
may be planted successfully in dishes, literally, if these are
deep enough for drainage pebbles and sufficient soil. Small
containers can be purchased with drainage holes and matching
saucers, if a more shallow planter is wanted.

A movable garden can have room for a landscaped scene.

In general, use of ornaments such as tiny animals, houses, and
pottery mushrooms is to be avoided in an indoor garden, unless
it is intended for a child. But in the very small garden, sometimes one thing may be used to build a simple scene around.
This should definitely fit the whole plan, size of plants, and
type of ground cover. It could be a rustic fence between two
clumps of miniature shrubbery that can be imagined to continue on beyond them. It could be a trellis for small-leaved
vines. Or in a garden planted formally with small flower beds,
it can be a miniature urn or tiny trough, with *Helxine soleirolii*
planted there and streaming down in diminutive trailers.

In the same way, a design may be built around a miniature
tree or a special flowering plant. The other plants would be
subdued in size and color, and fit the composition.

In these design arrangements featuring a plant or miniature
tree, the temptation sometimes is to overcrowd the planter.
Contrast in shape and color, on one hand, and the blending of
plants into a pattern, on the other, are played up better if there
is enough clear space and not too many conflicting elements.
Sometimes one plant in a small container is enough, or at most
two. When the shape of a small tree has character, and this is
enhanced by the slim trunk rising alone, then ground cover of
even small vines might be distracting. If something is wanted
besides the tree, one other small addition to the planting can
be used, as in Figure 23.

If there is room in the apartment or house for a temporary
placement box, as described in Chapter 9, or an inside window
box that can be bought at a hardware store, plants can be kept
there, with a basic supply of vines and creepers for ground
cover, and the small gardens can easily be altered and replanted
for a new appearance. This is convenient for changing the
effect for different purposes, such as changing the centerpiece
from a casual arrangement for a buffet, to a more stylized one
for a formal dinner. The transplanting should be done a couple
of days ahead when possible, to allow the plants to recover and
freshen up from transplanting, and the planter should be kept
moist and not in full sun for this period.

A design arrangement or a landscaped scene can be worked

out for specific occasions. A garden for the Christmas table, for example, would have dwarf holly, miniature evergreens, partridge-berry. Candles in holders shielded with green glass could be added, partially screened by foliage.

A landscaped garden can be fairly elaborate and still be carried and moved about easily, if most of the plants are small and likely to remain so. When a plan for the garden is worked out in detail on paper, it is easier to select appropriate plants. Suggestions for landscaping are scattered through these chapters, to be modified by personal preferences and the effect wanted for a room. The layout on paper is merely a basic plan, and changes often develop as the garden progresses. For example, when the planting starts, the effect may be too flat; then a hill is added; then a special plant is noticed in a greenhouse, that belongs under the hill, outlined against it.

If a garden is being developed for one room alone, there are advantages in making two matching gardens for that room. This is simplified by doing the basic work for both at the same time. Then one garden can be kept under the best possible conditions of sun, temperature, and humidity. The other can be used in its most effective place in the given room, to change places with its twin regularly.

When space and some carpentry are available, a place for the twin planter to find good growing and blooming conditions during northern winters is a window greenhouse. This, incidentally, is an attraction in itself.

The window greenhouse may be simple or elaborate, according to climate, amount of time and money to be spent, and whether or not it will be used as a major adjunct to a room. It may be a glass box built out from the window on supports, getting indoor heat through the open window, and protected in especially cold weather by padded coverings that can be made at home and tied on securely against wind. A greenhouse built just above the ground and opening out from a basement window of a house is another possibility. Either one can be designed to be removed for part of the year.

These window greenhouses may be purchased, ready to install. A do-it-yourself project is less expensive and can be planned to fit a specific location. The main things to consider are the sunny location, tight fitting of glass and framework, and coverings for cold nights or ice storms. A vent can be added, to be easily opened and closed for fresh air on mild days.

In addition to using the greenhouse for a twin planter, for any planter or potted plant needing sunlight, it makes a good place to propagate your own plants from seeds. This can be done in seed pans or in flowerpots. Various mixtures are used for soil, but unless there is a special requirement, general-purpose soil can be bought, all sterilized and sifted. Here you can grow things for special uses, from morning glory that will wind up the side of a cool window later, to the many plants that will take their places in miniature gardens and earn the comment, "I grew this myself from seed." These vary from something as simple as alyssum, to experiments and special interests.

The window greenhouse, like the temporary placement box, provides a store of change-material for planters: ivy of different lengths, moss in a well-watered pan, small foliage plants to be transplanted as wanted. Sometimes it isn't a flowering plant that is needed, but ground cover for a bare spot of soil, a plant to hold the line of a design where the original one is growing unevenly. Or sometimes precisely the right plant is found at a nursery to highlight in an additional planter, and this is simplified by having a store of greenery waiting to be combined with the new plant.

Added uses of the greenhouse as a supply source for planters include growing plants from cuttings or slips, encouraging speedy growth of a plant so it will fit a design, caring for a mystery plant someone gave you till you find out how it develops.

Design arrangements, as distinct from landscaped scenes in the planters, are sometimes easier but permit the same pleasure of working out steps toward a definite pattern. The final result is rewarding, with an effort more sophisticated and usually more aesthetically satisfying than the deployment of potted plants along a windowsill.

Among the many possibilities for design arrangement is a

Figure 8

Ted Budlong

A bromeliad, Cryptanthus zonatus zebrinus, *commonly called the zebra plant, is at the left.* Acorus *rises green and white at the center, and* Pilea depressa *wanders across the front.*

tropical planter. A miniature palm, or two of different heights, are placed first to dominate in outline. Tropical foliage plants are chosen according to the overall design. Bromeliads should have a prominent place here. Of these, certain members of the family, such as Billbergia (Figure 4), Cryptanthus (Figure 8), and Neoregelia (Figure 3), are more adaptable to light requirements. *Aechmeas* 'Foster's Favorite' (Figure 6), also adapts well. With interesting foliage as well as flowers, bromeliads repay attention to their individual needs in growing medium, whether compartmented soil, osmunda, or a mixture. The Cryptanthus in the oval planter has its own territory set apart with an underground wall.

Sometimes a more individual arrangement is gained by combining plants that haven't a relation to each other as in the tropical planter, except the relationship you establish in your pattern of line and color. Plants still in their pots can be tried in different positions till the pattern is decided.

In small planters, choice of vines and creeping plants for ground cover naturally is important because they show up clearly. *Pilea depressa* (Figure 8) has small leaves, spreads rapidly, and makes a change from *Helxine soleirolii* in these small containers.

To use and interchange small planters effectively when there is a large space available, perhaps on a sideboard, get several ceramic planters of the same color and shape but in different sizes. These may all be square, or round or oblong.

The planters are fitted with drainage holes and matching saucers. They are sold widely, sometimes as bonsai planters. And they are in subdued colors, tan or earthy brown, pale green or gray. Grouping them, there will be the repeated motif of their single shape. There should be at least one larger planter to hold the group together and give it focus. The arrangement of the small planters in a curved line, a more solid group, can be shifted daily. With extra planters to sun and exchange, there can be a design rising to high plants one day, and on another day all the planters would hold short plants and vines for a low spread of greenery.

A single small planter can be placed anywhere it's needed by installing a shelf to fit its size against the wall with brackets, or a triangular shelf across the corner of a room. Rosary vine makes a good showing here, if the shelf catches some sun. Otherwise vines that do well without sun can be used, such as two *Cissus* varieties, kangaroo vine or grape ivy.

For diversion as well as pleasant appearance, there is the citrus planter, where seedlings are featured that were grown at home from lemon and grapefruit seeds. These seeds should be planted shallowly in moist earth in a pot or pan and stay in a dark corner or covered till they show green. Soil should be checked meanwhile for moisture. With the sprouts showing well, the container is moved into light, and gradually as the seedlings mature, into full sunlight. One of my lemon seedlings is seen toward the back left in Figure 14, for height at three months.

Figure 9

Ted Budlong

A Chinese soup tureen of the medalion pattern with its vivid colors makes an interesting container for white begonia.

To specialize, with varieties of the same plant in containers placed about the room, gives a decorative linking. Miniature begonias offer a wide choice and opportunities for contrast in texture and color. Among the miniatures are 'China Doll,' 'Midget,' 'Chantilly Lace,' all rhizomatous, a division with many miniatures. Begonias are roughly divided into three classes, fibrous-rooted, rhizomatous, and tuberous-rooted, and branch out further in subdivisions—a massive family tree.

The wax begonias, semperflorens, of the fibrous-rooted division, flower well and adapt to average indoor temperature and lighting; their miniatures include 'Snowdrop,' 'Pandy,' and 'Pistachio.' Dwarf begonias or young plants of the larger varieties will fit the planter for a while till they must move on to larger space. In general, begonias do well in indoor gardens, as long as steps are taken to provide humidity. Suggestions have been made for this in other chapters.

If you want one large begonia plant, studded with flowers, to place among planters with miniatures or to stand by itself, don't leave it in its everyday pot. Somewhere around the house there will be a more interesting container, a quiet color for a bright-flowered plant, a container more definite in color and possibly more elaborate for a white-flowered plant. In my case, it turned out to be my grandmother's soup tureen for a white begonia (Figure 9).

Miniature roses are another choice for specialization, and will send visitors on a bemused tour of the room from planter to planter. They are more difficult to grow indoors than begonias, but with a little more time to provide the right conditions and care, especially if the climate permits a season outdoors or with windows wide open, they will grow and flower well. Regular watering and misting are vital. They should not stay permanently in an overheated room. They should be moved to the sun daily, or fluorescent light should be provided. Straggly growth should be pruned.

Though moisture is important to them, this can be worked out without too much trouble. Add some peat moss to the soil to retain moisture. Use one of the suggested devices such as humidity-pans hung behind radiators. Set a regular time each day for checking that the soil is moist. In a suspiciously dry room, check twice a day.

Miniature roses bloomed contentedly for me in a New York apartment, in a large planter known as "the farm." On winter days, when the radiators crackled busily and dryness mounted in the apartment, the roses would be apt to get an extra hasty misting as I went past on the run.

Names for miniature roses tend to be unfortunately cute; the roses deserve better. 'Bo-peep' has pink flowers and blooms well; if you miss a day's watering, a glance at its listless leaves will send you remedying the matter in a hurry. 'Red Imp' naturally has crimson flowers, and 'Pixie Gold' has yellow. As a final touch for this matter of names, a miniature rose, 'Miss Muffet,' has as parents 'Baby Bunting' and 'Tom Thumb.'

Movable planters that are easy to care for in a tight program can be filled with succulents. They need less watering; they don't mind dry air or reasonable changes of temperature.

Cacti are sometimes considered apart from other succulents, or sometimes all succulents are merged together with the cacti taking the lead. Actually cacti compose one quite separate branch of the succulents, with a center of growth peculiar to them called the areole. They combine well with other succulents, needing similar soil and care.

All succulents store moisture for use in dry periods. Their leaves and stems tend to be thick, and also juicy—which accounts for the name. Because of the desert climate of the normal location for most of them, they have taken on unusual characteristics for storage of water and protection against dry air.

Thus extraordinary shapes are found among the cacti and other succulents, which makes them unusual material for small planters. Some have closely piled fleshy leaves, some no leaves at all. Some are round, while the stone-plants resemble real stones. The window-plants live underground, sending up the tips of their leaves for sun.

In establishing a planter for succulents, a deep layer of drainage pebbles is important, as their roots should not stand in stagnant water. There should be sand in the soil mix. Various mixtures are used: a simple one is two parts sand, one part loam, one part leaf mold; another contains less sand, with crushed limestone and crushed brick used instead; another is three parts loam, three parts sand, and one part humus, with ground limestone added. The lines of the planter should be simple, not to conflict with the shapes of the plants.

The succulent garden should stand in sunlight or be moved to it daily. If full sun is too strong, this will be evident as leaves toward the sun will start to turn yellow.

Watering should be done sparingly. After succulents, especially cacti, are transplanted to the container, they should not be watered for a day or so. Then after the first watering, it will only be repeated when they show signs of needing it, such as a dry look about the stems. When they are watered, it should be done thoroughly, surplus water running off through drainage holes, or water given carefully to settle low in the pebbles. Intervals between watering will depend on climate and also on seasonal heating.

Cacti and other succulents should be shopped for personally if possible, to choose those with unusual appearance and to decide which will group well in a planter. Suggestions are the small cylinders of echinopsis; sand-dollars; rosary vine, mentioned earlier for a shelf by itself; small varieties of kalanchoe; rainbow bush; small aloes.

For another type of movable garden, when there is time in the program for frequent watering, very small plants in very small containers may be grouped together on a tray, for a garden look. Here individual pots, so-called, are part of the arrangement, and the accent is on diminutive effect, of both plants and pots.

The plants used are variously called miniature miniatures, thimble-size, or any phrase that accents smallness. They may be very young specimens, or one of the truly small plants.

The dramatic effect of using extremely small containers may be offset by the need to check for moisture and possibly to water several times a day. Watering is done with an eyedropper, and also by misting the plants that like water on their leaves. You might collect small containers, anything around the house that is small enough; an example is the top of a travel-size tube of cold cream. Further suggestions for containers will be found in Chapter 13. Plant an experimental small container with something relatively unimportant, even an infant clover you picked up on a walk. Then see if the watering outweighs the amusement value.

If so, small plants may still be used, with an arrangement of them placed in their own small terrarium. Sometimes an open-top terrarium will work out, as suggested in Chapter 9, using a glass bowl or deep wine glass. It can be covered part of the time, to cut down the need for watering.

Certain miniature plants often deserve placement alone. One of these is a bromeliad, *Tillandsia ionantha,* with the popular name of Little Hedgehog. It is an air plant, and can spend part of its time on a curl of bark in its small planter, and then move, bark and all, to be a decorative addition to a large terrarium (Figure 13). It should be misted frequently, once a day if the air is dry and it isn't protected by glass.

Sinningia pusilla, a gesneriad (Figure 27), is another plant that shows well alone. The tiny green leaves make a rosette against the soil. Fragile violet-pink flowers rise on long, slender stems. It should have water regularly to keep the soil lightly moist. And it is fed with a solution that sounds like a starvation diet, one-fifth of a teaspoon of nutrient to a gallon of water, but it thrives and flowers on this.

To return to relatively larger miniatures for movable gardens, the greenhouses and florist shops are carrying them in growing numbers, but it's a good plan to check ahead by phone to be sure what is available. You have a wide choice if you order by mail, and sources of supply are listed at the back of the book. An excellent source is Merry Gardens, carrying foliage and flowering plants with many specialties. Their catalog is keyed to a culture guide, useful for example if you are going to grow bromeliads for the first time and want to be sure of the proper care for each you order.

Sometimes you may order flowers to combine for a planter, and when they arrive, find one so well proportioned and characterful that you will use it singly. The right container

Figure 10

Ted Budlong

Peperomia astrid *'Pixie' fits under the larger leaves of* Dracaena godseffiana *'Florida Beauty,' with* Helxine soleirolii *for ground cover, and a small slip of* Peperomia rubella *at the right front.*

for a single miniature is just as important as that for a land-scaped scene. It should not be so large the plant is islanded, or so small the plant looks cramped even if it isn't. And the appearance of container and plant should harmonize, making a design together.

Sometimes, again, you can fit together several elements of plant and container. The farthest I have gone in this direction was in using the bowl of an 1804 tea set as a container. The bowl was the maidenhair fern pattern, with a tiny motif in green against the white. So of course it was planted with maidenhair fern alone, not only because the foliage pattern repeated that of the bowl, but also because both ferns and bowl combined delicacy with simplicity, and because the curves of the fronds followed curves of the bowl (Figure 1).

Movable planters can easily be taken to the kitchen or to a work table for grooming and changes in the planting. They can follow the sun from window to window. They can be very small, or the medium size of the average so-called dish garden (Figure 10), or as large as can be managed comfortably.

Their character is a matter of choice. But their adaptability is an important point in their favor.

7. Herb Gardens

TWO HERB GARDENS, FOR KITCHEN AND DINING ROOM, PLACE THE herbs within easy reach and make attractive displays. The kitchen garden, of course, has herbs at hand for cooking. In the dining room garden are herbs for salads, desserts, and drinks.

The dining room garden, on a side table or wide shelf at a window, has accessories that make an interesting effect as well as playing their part in events. Just as salad often is mixed and the dressing prepared at the table at home or in a restaurant, so the addition of herbs from the nearby garden to the salad on the dining room table, just before it is tossed, has the values of novelty and last-minute freshness. Here the accessories come into use.

There will be long, thin-bladed scissors on the side table, to cut the herbs wanted, and to trim woody stems. A mortar and pestle set stands ready for crushing leaves. There should be a small wooden chopping bowl, with its curved-blade knife. So the final touch to a salad is given when you reach for chives or chervil from the garden and chop them. Toss them in the salad, with a fresh scent in the air as well as a fresh taste in the salad.

Herbs for salads, in addition to chives and the more difficult chervil, include basil, mustard, and possibly burnet. Nasturtiums offer leaves and seed pods, and sometimes the flowers are used in salads as well as being decoration for the garden.

This dining room garden is planted for landscaping values as well as use. So herbs may be added for visual effect, such as rosemary with its attractive foliage. Parsley makes good greenery, and is handy for a final garnish for a platter.

Figure 11

Ted Budlong

In the kitchen herb garden here the taller herbs at the back, from left to right, are winter savory, basil, rosemary and mint. In front, again from left, are thyme, chives, marjoram, and parsley.

Mints are important here: peppermint, curly mint, applemint, for desserts and drinks. There is also borage for the bar department. These grow tall, and can be at the ends of the garden, or in pots behind the planter.

The kitchen herb garden may be small, for personally chosen herbs (Figure 11). It may be a long planter, with herbs that need varying amounts of water in their separate pots sunk in the soil. The garden should be in a sunny window if possible. Other herbs above in hanging baskets, such as Italian oregano, conserve space and add to the effect. Larger herbs, tall or sometimes tending to straggle, can be in pots on a pebble-and-water tray behind the planter.

Kitchen herbs have fascinating varieties of flavor, as all imaginative cooks know. There can be sweet basil and sweet marjoram, the adjective referring to the aroma and not the taste. Rosemary and winter savory are found in the kitchen garden, in pots screened behind the planter. Sage and thyme are familiar flavor names.

Two-way herbs, those which may be used in both gardens, include tarragon, chervil, mint, and basil. Dwarf-bush basil is attractive for the dining room. Chives in the dining room can be used sparingly, with an eye for the garden effect, and chives in the kitchen garden used more lavishly.

Sweet marjoram, or *Maporana hortensis,* is one of the medieval strewing herbs, nowadays used for vegetables, meats, and fish. Pot marjoram, *Origanum onites,* has a stronger flavor; it has the same uses and is at home in Italian and Spanish dishes.

Some herbs will be included in the gardens mainly for their appearance or for special purposes. In considering their use for flavor, everyone will have individual preferences. Part of the fun of these gardens is having the special herbs one likes fresh at hand, as well as experimenting. Some categories of cooking herbs are mentioned here as suggestions, in case they may be overlooked.

These include herbs for hors d'oeuvres, soups and stews, meats and fish, vegetables, cheese dishes, egg dishes, and desserts. There are also the herb butters and sauces, uses of a bouquet garni, and herb vinegars for salads and cooking.

For hors d'oeuvres, hot sage biscuits can be split and spread with butter and grated cheese; a half teaspoon of the herb is used for the regular recipe. Herb puffs, quickly made for unexpected company with sharp cheese cut to fit small squares of bread, are sprinkled with winter savory and put under the broiler. Chicken livers are broiled with wine and your own mixture of chopped green herbs.

Among the cold soups are cucumber and chives, or water-cress soup, prepared in the blender with parsley. For hot soups and stews, individual choices will decide. A bouquet garni can be made of three or four sprigs of herbs tied together, to be removed after cooking. For instance, basil, parsley, and thyme; basil, parsley, and chives; chervil, parsley, and chives.

Meats and fish can be combined with all kitchen herbs at one time and another. During cooking, there is the bouquet garni; a court bouillon for fish, with your favorite herbs chosen; and for roasts, garlic and rosemary for lamb, sage for pork. An occasional use of herbs is the marinade, in which the meat remains overnight; the marinade then will be used for basting. Chicken adapts well to many herbs, broiled with garlic, rose-mary, basil, thyme or tarragon, or a pinch of sage. The liquid with which the chicken is basted during cooking, which con-tains the herbs, can be stock, wine, or sour cream. Herb brandy is used on steaks, chops, and fish. Pesto, a garlic and basil sauce, used for meats and pasta, only really tastes like pesto when freshly crushed basil is used. And for after cooking, there are the herb butters and sauces.

Your own preference should decide the selection of herbs for seasoning vegetables. There are marjoram or chives for green vegetables; chopped mixed herbs for boiled onions; as a change from parsley and chives for potatoes, try other inter-esting flavors.

Chives, winter savory and basil, alone or in combination, are added to cheese and egg dishes. A soufflé, with a delicate touch of herb flavor, is a diversion from savory omelets. Eggs benedict are improved by a chopped herb garnish. Quiche gives an opportunity for more definitely flavored herbs.

Fruit desserts are accented by leaves of rose geranium or lemon verbena. For cold-weather desserts, canned peaches and pears may be poached with fresh mint. Mint is more familiar for summer desserts, with cantaloupe or fresh fruit cup. One of my favorites for a very hot evening is a dessert of honey-dew melon balls in crème de menthe and fresh mint.

Suggestions are included here for herb brandy and herb vinegars. Herb brandy may be used on broiled meats, fowl, or fish, a few drops shaken on during or after cooking. It can be made in quantity, sealed in small, attractive bottles, and used as gifts. A pint of brandy is poured over half a cup of crushed basil, thyme, marjoram, mint, or rosemary as preferred; this should stand two weeks and then be strained; the same brandy can then be poured over another half-cup of leaves, to provide greater strength.

Herb vinegar can be made from white or red wine vinegar or malt vinegar. To make the herb vinegar, fill a jar full of bruised herbs, add a cup of vinegar which has been heated to a boil, then add cold water till the jar is filled, and let stand for two weeks. Then pour off through a strainer, and seal in bottles to be stored ready for use. Basil or garlic combine well with red wine vinegar, tarragon or mint with white wine vinegar. A row of bottles of the various flavors along a kitchen shelf is ready for use, and the different ones can be combined later if desired.

In the kitchen garden or dining room garden, there are further herbs to be added, offering different qualities of fragrance, visual effect, special uses, and traditional associations. These include lavender, of course, to be dried for drawers and linen closet. Camomile is good for foliage, and perhaps for traditions of medicinal use—and Peter Rabbit. Some scented-leaved geraniums and lemon verbena can be included for fragrance. Horehound is an herb with a name that has reminiscent flavor. Burnet has leaves with a delicate taste of cucumber, to be used for flavoring.

A special division of herb garden might be considered for catnip, if there is a cat on the premises. This has interesting if distracting possibilities. It might be better to grow this from seeds rather than from small plants, according to old herb lore, to achieve a reasonable growth without cat interference. The old saying goes:

> If you sow it, the cat won't know it
> If you set it, the cat will get it

Some basic points for the establishment and care of herb gardens start with the sunny location, and with a soil that is on the alkaline side and is not too rich. The soil can be a mixture of sandy loam and Black Magic African violet mix, or regular potting soil. Roots of the herbs shouldn't stand in water, so a deep layer of drainage pebbles is indicated in the planters; also pebbles in the tall-rimmed saucers or trays under potted herbs with water kept below the bottom of the pots as usual. When the weather is mild, nearby windows should be opened.

The perennial herbs benefit from being placed outdoors part of the time in mild climates or during summer in the North. Bring most of them in well before frost, though mints, chives, and tarragon should stay out till frosted.

Herbs tend to discourage insects. But if pests do develop, so that spraying with insecticide is considered, the only course is—don't. Better to cut back the affected plants or replace them with a fresh supply, rather than to spray with DDT and to make a mental note about washing the herbs later—a note that can't be followed thoroughly enough.

Herbs should be watered according to their preferences and as the dryness of the soil indicates. Misting can be done in addition, particularly for rosemary.

Herb gardens are maintained indefinitely, with feeding, changing of soil annually, repotting, renewal of annuals, a seasonal shift outdoors, and the pruning that is necessary. Additions will make a change in appearance of the gardens, as well as providing experimental material in new flavors, and sometimes proving that still another herb will settle down indoors.

The gardens literally provide garden-fresh flavor and the pleasure of using your own home-grown herbs. They make attractive additions to dining room and kitchen. And small mint plants may be removed by root division as they grow thickly, or a clump of chives may be taken from the kitchen garden, to be planted in tiny pots and given to guests to take away as a start for further herb gardens.

8. Rock Gardens

THE INDIVIDUAL QUALITIES OF ROCK GARDENS CAN BE DRAMATIZED indoors. A rock garden for your living room is easy to make, and the design can be altered for a new effect as the weeks pass.

To get the most interesting results and have scope for special planning, this garden should be built on three levels. The finished small scene will have two terraces, their vines cascading down to the foreground, with its grotto or pool.

The container for the rock garden can be an oblong box, its sides high enough to rise two inches above the tallest terrace. But a better effect will be gained from a box with its two sides slanting down from back to front, giving a good view from three directions and a more airy look. This type of planter is shown in Figure 12. It can be made of galvanized metal, by a tinsmith, and painted a subdued color. Or a wooden box can easily be cut down as illustrated, made waterproof as explained in Chapter 9, and stained.

In preparing this garden, the matter of rocks should be considered early, with time to select them carefully. Otherwise when you start planting you may have a boring collection of rocks on hand. Keep a basket handy in which to drop interesting rocks as you find them, and also what you have previously thought of as pebbles. As you go about, consider small stones as if you looked at them through a magnifying glass. Pebbles take on new character, and a three-inch stone will be a huge boulder in your miniature garden.

Stones should have interesting shapes, with slopes and peaks. In general, the stones and small rocks you collect should be of the same general type, perhaps fieldstone, or somewhat the same tones of gray, so the effect will hold together. If you want one contrasting stone, a creamy color, or a rock streaked with quartz, this can eventually be partly covered by vines, so it will show but not dominate.

For country dwellers in most parts of the country, a rock hunt is easy. City people can collect enough potential rocks on

Figure 12

Ted Budlong

The rock garden illustrated has miniature trees, described in this chapter, on the middle and top levels, with the soil left clear below them. Vines are growing down toward the grotto at the front left, but in this garden the plants are kept more separate than in the closely planted waterfall garden, to show their character and also the rock shapes.

one day's trip to the country, or can find them in areas where a building is being torn down and the chips of granite lie about for the choosing. When rocks or the time to collect them are in short supply, a variety may be ordered by mail.

An all-purpose soil may be obtained from a florist or garden supply store, or taken from a garden bed. You may want to work out your own mixture. If you plan to use a plant that requires a special type of soil, then in addition to its isolation in a rock pocket, use a barrier of foil or slate or thin rock underground, as mentioned earlier.

Your planter may have drainage holes stopped with corks, or a deeper layer of drainage pebbles. These pebbles, placed at the bottom with a mixture of crushed charcoal, should be an inch deep with drainage holes and two inches without them. You can see the sudden importance of pebbles, both for drainage and for use on the surface.

When you start to landscape, cover the drainage pebbles with two to three inches of soil. This will complete the foreground, with the earth at least an inch below the edge of the planter. Mark off four inches of foreground with toothpicks, to show where you will start the first slope. From there to the back, build up the earth two inches higher. Use about an inch back-to-front for a steep slope to the center terrace.

Here you will need a retaining wall of rocks, most of them buried, a few showing sides or top. Use large enough rocks so the slope will hold firm when watered, while the vines take hold. Your slope to center level, then, rising about two inches, is solidly constructed of rocks, with earth placed about them.

If you are going to have a grotto, this should be planned now, and rocks placed for it, perhaps with the terrace higher at this point. Directions are given later for a grotto, with other special effects.

On the center level, sink rocks to form pockets for the larger plants you will put there. The tops of these rocks will show above the surface, placed to make a pleasant design.

Rocks should be set slanting, bottom toward the back, so water will go toward the soil and roots. In building the pockets for individual plants, slant the rocks in toward where the roots will be so water will be directed the same way. Two or three pockets are enough for the center level, as you will need space for vines, and can always change your design at a later date.

Some of the rocks on the center level can extend back where the next rise will be, and will be covered by earth. So you have plenty of scope for generous pockets. Be sure to allow enough space for future growth of roots. The center level, when completed, will have two or three deepish holes for pockets, with rocks placed about them. Width of this terrace will be about three inches, front to back.

The second rise is again steep, taking about an inch front-to-back, again rising about two inches, and shored up firmly as before with rocks. But here you should vary your slope so it won't look stolid. In one or two places, let the slope be more gradual, cutting into the top terrace. In all instances, the larger part of the rock will be underground. But here and there, on the top slope and top terrace, allow more of a rock to show, choosing those with interesting shapes. After all, this is a rock garden, and the rocks add effect as well as doing construction work.

On both slopes, after placing rocks and soil, use a quantity of pebbles set into the earth firmly, to hold it in place while it is settling. This will save trouble the first few days in repairing washouts after watering. As vines advance, pebbles can be removed.

There are about two inches left, of the one-foot side dimension, above the top terrace. This terrace will be irregular, according to how you made your slope, and the soil will be broken here and there by a portion of rock showing above the surface. On the front edge you might have a V of rocks, or a rock with a sharp depression in the top, where vines will pour through toward the slope.

Again you will want two or three pockets, according to the number of plants you plan to use at the start on the top terrace. The earth of the level portion should fall at least an inch below the top of the planter, to allow for easy watering. Pockets here will be smaller in width than those on the center terrace but have good depth. If there is one larger plant you wish to use on the top terrace, allow for its larger pocket by breaking into the slope with a rock arrangement.

This top terrace will have an interesting broken line at the front edge, with its boulders and varying slope. The two rises or slopes to the two terraces can be planned to your choice, with a contrast between a perpendicular line of rock, and a more gradual slope of earth and rock and pebbles. As you work, imagine where the vines will clamber down for best effect, and allow for them.

With the two terraces and their slopes completed, dampen the earth carefully, and watch for any place that needs a more solid rock construction to hold the earth in place. Add pebbles generously for temporary holding.

This garden has character, at this point, before the first plant is set in. Study it to appraise the overall arrangement, the amount of rocks showing, a sufficiently varied line of slopes and terraces.

Plants should have been collected by this time, from nurseries, shippers, or your own seed pans.

Before any planting is done, set pots containing the larger plants about the landscape, making sure you like their positions. At least one plant should rise high from the center level, extending well above the top terrace. At least two larger plants, with others of varying heights, should be placed to partially screen the top or back edge of the planter, on the top terrace. Later you can persuade some vines to go up and over this back edge. As you study the effect, you will probably want to use the largest plants at the bottom or center levels, but one tall plant or miniature tree may add interest to the top terrace. This study of the final arrangement, while you can change the pots around and try different choices, is very important for this garden. With three levels to play with, you can work out interesting landscaping.

When at last you start planting, you can work with the larger plants first as selected for all three levels, or do the main part of the planting on the top level. In either case, you will probably get a new idea as you go, and take out a rock or make a new pocket. The moist earth should handle well, and don't worry that there is a scattering of earth on the rocks, as they can be washed off last of all. Your main design will hold firm, and changes are part of creating a garden.

If you are undecided about the placement of a plant, leave it temporarily in the pot, with the rim covered, so you can easily switch it later. But as far as possible, put the larger plants in permanent position.

One or two miniature trees will be effective on the terraces. Many of these trees prefer a cold winter, so check when you buy or order them so that your trees will have a good chance to live happily indoors. If you don't keep the thermostat pushed to the 80 degree mark in winter, you can experiment more widely. The illustrated rock garden shows a spruce, *Picea glauca conica*, one of the miniature trees that should do well indoors, and a cypress, *Chamaecyparis lawsoniana forsteckiana*. Various dwarf conifers have been grown successfully indoors, so if you find one that you can't bear to leave behind, try it in your rock garden. If the line blurs between dwarf and miniature, and the tree you want can be expected to grow inches taller than you wish, be discouraging in the amount of space you allow for the roots.

After the important plants are set out on top and second terrace, there should be enough irregularity of ground for interest. You can have a mound of higher ground on one of the terraces—preferably at a side rather than in the center—held in place by rocks. And here make a mental note that a plant in raised position should be checked for moisture when watering, unless you have a fairly tight pocket under it. If the tops of rocks break the line sufficiently, then the ground of the terraces can be more level.

Your original overall design, in imagination or on paper, can be changed later. You can try one arrangement, and after your plants are thriving, alter the design and interchange plants. But the original design should be allowed to stand for at least a week, and the plants should not be moved about on planting day after they are removed from their pots. A plant can eventually take moving, without being discomposed, when this is done carefully with earth about the roots. The main point is to allow enough time before doing this. You will find that some plants settle in at once, with new foliage starting, while others need more time to adjust to transport and planting.

In selecting what you will plant, consider that ferns and mosses combine well with rocks. A dwarf fern, *Polystichum tsus-simense*, tends to remain low. This will need misting. Look at the small ferns available in nurseries, to find some you like. Many interesting varieties can be ordered from suppliers' catalogs. *Pellaea adiantoides* is a dwarf form of holly fern. Small versions of the larger ferns can be used, trimmed back, and eventually removed and potted for a gift. Some wild ferns, taken small enough with a ball of earth around their roots, can be coaxed into healthy indoor life. Club moss and other varieties can be purchased. Or you may like to find your own in the woods, often near a stream.

Some heaths and heathers adapt well to an indoor garden, if the temperature is not kept too warm. They may need to retire for a period to a cool part of the house.

Vines are of top importance, to stream down from the terraces. Here is the place for ivy. Some of the English ivies are not true miniatures, but can be trimmed as desired. Needlepoint, a real miniature, may be used when you want a long torrent of small-leaved vine. Look at various ivies for a selection, such as 'Green Feather.' One of the miniature ivies, 'Merion Beauty,' has interesting leaves. You will encourage the early effect of your rock garden if some of the ivy already has started to trail and can be started in the right direction down a slope. The amount of vines used will depend on whether you want the final effect to be a mass of greenery as shown in the photograph of the waterfall garden, which has several levels, or whether you want individual plants and trees to stand out clearly. In the rock garden illustrated, no vines are planted near the miniature trees on top and middle levels.

Check your catalogs for vines you like. Lay in a good supply of *Helxine soleirolii*. A good trailer is called Kenilworth ivy, and is really *Cymbalaria muralis*.

Foliage and flowering plants for all three levels are for your choice, in individual effect or combination. You have an array to choose from, in catalogs or greenhouses. Be sparing in your selection at the start, because the basic charm of the rock garden should be the terraced effect, the rocks and vines, with plants set here and there as accents. Too many plants will clog the terraces and blur the total effect.

You may want to start with only miniature trees, ferns, and vines for the terraces, and use other plants for the bottom level. Perhaps you have miniature geraniums or roses, in small pots set on pebbles, and want to transfer them to the rock garden. They can be left in their pots, sunk in earth, for a time, while you find if they get sufficient sun in the window where you have placed the rock garden. They can be tested out, and removed if they need a change of scene.

In the foreground, or bottom level, there can be a more dramatic use of rocks. You can make a tiny grotto, dug in under the middle terrace. This should be constructed when that terrace is made, with a flat stone set across two side walls of rock. Soil will be spread over the top, which will then be part of the middle terrace, with vines running across and dripping down partly shielding the top of the grotto. Plants in your bottom level can conceal the supporting stones as desired. Make the grotto large enough so it can contain a tiny fern, a pile of white pebbles, or a planting of small vine that runs on outside. This will not only vary the rising ground between bottom and middle levels, but will make a drama point for the foreground.

The foreground is the place for your most interesting boulder, sunk partly into the ground, with a fern rising behind it. Or make a slanting pile of pebbles and small stones, with some *Helxine soleirolii* set in earth at the top, to finger its way down.

A better unity is gained if the special features of the foreground have some relationship to the slope behind them— either rock continuing out from the slope at one point, the grotto and its planting left with plenty of space around it so it will be featured, or vines and pebbles continuing out from the slope to a boulder on the bottom level.

If you find a rock with a crevice for planting, or if you chisel out space in a rock for earth, you can have a vine or small plant that seems to grow out of the rock. Moss covering the earth adds to this effect. Or rocks piled together can conceal a planting space, where you could put *Tradescantia multiflora*, a miniature creeping plant, or a small-leaved philodendron.

A feature of the foreground could be a small rock wall at one side. You can put together tiny stones, fitting and balancing them into a wall, which can be tidy or wander casually. In crevices of the wall put creeping and crevice plants. This is a good place for pussy-toes (*Antennaria*).

A pool can be used in the foreground, with small rocks and pebbles leading to it from the slope. Here you put flat bits of rock, with lichen if you're lucky, to set around the pool and slant irregularly across the rim. Any bare spots of rim can be covered with moss. A tiny bowl or deep ash tray can be used for a pool, always of a color that suits a woodland pool effect.

During the landscaping, though most of the work is done from the low front, be sure to check the sides once in a while. Foliage or rocks should rise above the sides, from the terraces and foreground, to invite the observer over for a closer look. The earth, however, should always be a little below the slanting sides, or there will be a watering problem.

Planting can be adjusted, according to the size planter used. Directions are given here, on a basis of a foot and a half in width, a foot in depth, and a foot in height. The two points to consider in working out measurements are the slanting sides and sufficient height to allow for the terraces.

Last step of the planting is to check if ground cover is needed in some bare spots. While this is growing and spreading, you can sprinkle around small stone chips, which look better than bare earth, and help hold moisture in.

Make sure the soil is firm around all the plants. Sprinkle water on carefully where the ground is not moist enough.

Now stand back and look. The vines have yet to spread down the terraces lushly, but already they look as if they had always lived there. Rocks are half concealed by greenery, rising here and there to stand clear. The terraces give a special depth and dimension, a quality all their own. In this short time, you have an indoor rock garden.

9. Terrariums

A MINIATURE GREENHOUSE FOR MINIATURE PLANTS CAN BRING an enclosed green world to your own side table. It is a garden under glass, living its life apart, while you watch the slow changes: a fern unfolding, a vine reaching, and perhaps one morning when you come down to breakfast, your first tiny orchid in bloom.

These glass containers—terraria, usually called terrariums— are fun to make and plant, as well as to enjoy afterward. They are most effective when they are landscape-gardened in small scale, to provide a tropical scene, a tiered vista, an arrangement with interesting combinations in shape and color. They can be as individual as you choose, with your personal mark on them.

A terrarium is a dramatic addition to any room. It will brighten a window that has a dull outlook, glamorize a room divider, be a conversation piece on the coffee table. Set on a table with casters, it can be moved about from room to room, catching sun in the morning, and later shining under a light in a dark hall.

Each such enclosed garden we make, whether it's as small

Figure 13

Ira Finke
Donald H. Clark

This terrarium is planted for a tropical effect, with leaves and fronds close together and vines spreading lushly. Miniature gesneriads add flowers and interesting leaves. Smithiantha zebrina 'Little One' *blooms at the center front, and* Achimenes andrieuxii *is in flower at the right front corner. There is an open space at the left, in front of the fern and palm. Here is a marshy corner for the pitcher plant, and room for a log and a curl of bark. On the bark is a miniature bromeliad,* Tillandsia ionantha, *silvery green, with its offshoot. In the lower photograph, showing this corner and taken three weeks earlier,* Sinningia pusilla *is in flower above the log.*

Figure 14

Ira Finke
Donald H. Clark

Except for the miniature orchids at the back, and maidenhair fern rising at the right, the planting of this terrarium is kept low, to show a small landscape centering around the pool. In the larger photograph, Koellikeria erinoides *and the sinningias are coming into bud. In the lower photograph,* Columnea 'Joy' *is in bloom at the back left;* Sinningia concinna *flowers at the right front corner next to S. pusilla; and a hybrid,* Sinningia 'Bright Eyes' *above the pool.* Selaginella kraussiana *makes a green tracery at the front and around the pool.*

as a wine glass or long as a radiator, is new and our own. But the general plan has been around for quite a while.

The origin of the terrarium is often credited to Dr. N. B. Ward, a London surgeon of the nineteenth century, though some minor credit might also be given to a cocoon. Between them, they developed a sealed glass case for plants, which held its own humid climate by conserving and condensing moisture. The story goes that Dr. Ward accidentally discovered the principle of growing plants in a tight case when he put the cocoon of a sphinx moth on moist earth in a glass bottle and closed the bottle with a piece of metal. Within a short time a fern and grasses appeared in the unopened bottle. Dr. Ward seems to have lost all interest in the cocoon, which disappeared from the story, and instead watched the plant life in the closed container, which grew contentedly without any care for four years.

After this, various forms of glassed, closed containers, called Wardian cases, were used in transporting plants through differing climate zones, and adapted for home use in various countries. But though Dr. Ward's name was given to them, this was not the earliest type of terrarium. The establishment of a humid atmosphere for growing plants by the use of glass containers was known some twenty-five hundred years ago in Greece, where glass jars were used for this purpose.

Terrarium history in this country may be said to have started with the squaw bowls of New England housewives. Partridge-berry plants were kept during the winter, embedded in moss, in these glass squaw bowls.

Technically, a terrarium is tightly closed. But in present varied use, they may be closed; or constructed so air can be admitted part of the time; or with glass sides but no top, which provides enough humidity for many plants that don't like dry air.

The second type, which allows fresh air as desired, is a good selection for most purposes. It does not have the factor of condensed moisture on the glass, frequently cutting down the view, which is common to the closed cases. It requires less care than the open-top type. And it permits a large selection of interesting plants and adjustments from closed top to fresh air, according to room humidity, conditions in the case, and personal program.

Terrariums not only are very effective, but also enable us to bring into the house or apartment a variety of plants that would not adapt well to an open planter and the rather dry air of many homes. Also, they are attractive to busy people, because they may be left unattended for some time. If you are going away for the weekend, you can check whether your terrarium needs a misting with a judicious amount of water and the earth is correctly moist, then close the top, forget it, and find it waiting in good condition when you return.

Preparing a terrarium can be done over a period of time using a spare hour here and there, with an afternoon for the planting. Certain things should be done early, however, so that the terrarium case will not stand ready to be planted while there is a frustrating lack of one vital item.

First of all, it is important to decide where the finished terrarium will stand most of the time, so that its size can be determined. Next decide what sort of final effect you want— for example, a small landscape with featured plants, set with plenty of space between for moss and tiny vines and creeping plants for ground cover, or a lush tropical scene more closely planted. These points may affect your next choice.

Are you going to buy a terrarium case, or build one yourself? If limited time is a factor, perhaps you'll want to order a terrarium case from catalogs of firms listed at the back of this book. Here you will of course be restricted as to size and shape, and the material used with the glass is apt to be a shiny metal.

If you like to make things, or have a member of the family interested in simple carpentry work, it is much more rewarding to have your own case. You can choose a size exactly right for the room or table. You will have a finished product that combines wood with glass, which makes a subdued frame allowing the plants and flowers to dominate. And you can have some added special features, which we have worked out for specific needs and described below.

Some authorities suggest that a terrarium can be made by using an old fish tank or round fish bowl, covered with a glass top. This is of course practical. The trouble is, the terrarium will continue, even when planted, to resemble an old fish tank or round fish bowl. Once again, a more individual solution pays off in final effect.

Two terrarium cases are suggested here, for a family or personal project. The first is very inexpensive and quickly made. The finished case is shown in Figure 13. The second costs a bit more and takes longer to make, but achieves more. This case is shown in Figure 14.

To make the first case, you start with a shallow box, for example a flat from a nursery. This should be three to four inches deep. The flat in the illustration cost nothing, and was chosen for its size and new condition. If you do not intend to keep the terrarium on a tray, the box must be made watertight. You have a choice of materials here. If you haven't met "handi-patch," a device that spans swiftly any size of hole in your wooden box, you might like a formal introduction at your hardware store. This will take care of the space between boards of a flat, the cracks of a box. There is also caulking material for the same purpose. When your box is watertight, if you want to keep it that way for a longer period, coat the inside of the box with a commercial rot preventative. The finished box should be stained, dark or light as you prefer.

Now that the bottom of the case is completed, you next have the glass sides cut at a glazier's or hardware store; the thickness of ordinary window glass is quite satisfactory. The terrarium illustrated was made with glass twelve inches high. Four panes of glass should be cut each with a height of twelve inches; two will have as their length the exact length of the inside of your box, the other two will have for length the inner width of the box minus two thicknesses of the glass, which allows for fitting inside the long pieces. A fifth piece of glass should be cut one-quarter inch larger than the box dimensions on all sides, for the top.

The four glass panes for the sides are set firmly into a strip of caulking material along the bottom inside edges of the box.

The corners are taped. As illustrated, brown plastic tape was used to match the stained bottom. The fifth pane is taped at the sides, for handling in removing the top.

Actual working time for this terrarium case is less than two hours. The cost of the glass is about $2.50, according to local rates.

The second suggested terrarium was planned to meet a number of preferences and needs. For example, some terrariums are square, which limits the interesting landscapes that can be made. Some have such a deep base that the total effect is clumsy, or are too high for good proportions, or have a solid top that makes the effect heavy and doesn't give the preferably airy look. Small feet were wanted which would be unobtrusive but allow neat handling of corks in drainage holes. In particular, a top was worked out which would not be as readily dislodged as a piece of glass resting on the sides; which would open easily for differing amounts of fresh air; and which would conform to the total design. Anyone with a reasonable assortment of tools should be able to complete it easily. (See diagrams, Figure 15.)

The following materials are needed:

lumber:
    1 piece of ¾" plywood 16" x 11"
    10 feet of ¾" square stock
    5 feet of 1" x 2" stock (actual size ¾" x 1⅝")
    45 feet of ¼" quarter round molding
glass:
    2 panes 10$^{15}/_{16}$" x 15$^{15}/_{16}$" for front and back
    2 panes 10$^{15}/_{16}$" square for sides
    1 pane 12" x 16¾" for top
brads
glue (such as Elmer's or other which dries clear)
stain
rot preventative
four small rubber "feet"

Any good lumberyard will have the wood. The rest can be

obtained at a hardware store. Total cost is about ten dollars: $5 for the lumber, $2.50 for the glass, $1.50 each for stain and rot-proof, the other items about a dollar. The exact cost depends on whether you have stain, brads, and glue on hand.

Get the lumber dealer to cut the ¾″ plywood exactly; if you want to be safe and sure, buy a slightly larger piece and cut it yourself. This is your base. You should then cut the ¾″ square stock into four 13⅜″ pieces for corners, two 16″, and two 11″ pieces for the top frame. The 1″ x 2″ stock is cut into two 16″ and two 11″ pieces to frame the bottom. The quarter

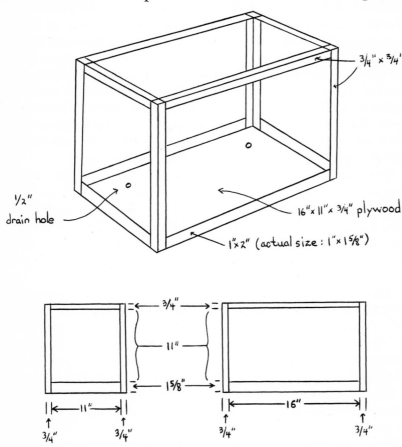

Figure 15

round is used to hold in the glass on the front, back, and sides, and also to frame the sliding glass top. Cut sixteen 15½" sections for the corners, eight 11" sections for the sides, and eight 16" sections for the front and back. (If possible, cut the ends of these pieces at a 45° angle, as in a picture frame. You will then cut the quarter round into twenty-four 11" pieces and eight 16" pieces.) Then cut one 17½" and two 12¼" lengths of quarter round to frame the top on three sides.

Stain all the pieces and allow to dry at least overnight. Drill two drain holes in the base, about three inches from each end, so that if you ever need to drain out a surplus of water, this can be done by turning the terrarium so one end with drain hole is off the table. These holes are to be filled with corks, whittled to size.

Glue and nail the bottom framing to the base. Then attach the corner posts and the top framing in the same manner. Make sure all the corners are right angles, and that the rectangular frame formed by the corner posts and top framing presents an even surface for the glass on top to slide upon. Allow the glue to dry thoroughly, at least for several hours.

You are now ready to install the glass. Place all the inside framing of quarter rounds. Use a generous amount of glue and wipe off the excess; small brads *may* also be used, though they should be tapped very gently. Especially if you use only glue, allow it to dry thoroughly. Then set each piece of glass in place and glue the outside framing of quarter rounds. (See diagrams, Figure 15.)

Glue the 17½" and 12¼" quarter round strips to the rectangle formed by the corner posts and top framing. The one side is left without a framing piece to allow the glass to slide back an inch or so for ventilation. If the edges of the glass are sharp, cover the back edge with brown plastic tape for easier handling.

Paint the inside of the base and the insides of the bottom framing with rot preventative. Cork the drain holes, and you're all set.

If you have time and space, you might consider making an extra-watertight box, like the base of the first terrarium, without the glass. This would be used as a temporary placement box. It has many purposes, such as a place to put newly acquired plants briefly till you settle them in the terrarium; a place to grow plants that need less humidity till they are the size you prefer for the open garden or terrarium; a place in which to sink small pots of plants which need pruning or other special attention before final placement. A baking pan can be used for this purpose also, or one of the solid plastic flats sold in stores handling garden materials.

Incidentally, if you have or locate a baking pan, such as an oblong cake pan, which has straight sides with no flare, and sharp instead of rounded corners, this can be used as an inexpensive bottom for the first terrarium. It is not, however, as aesthetically satisfactory as the wooden base described.

There are two points to note on a time schedule for your terrarium preparations. The first is the acquiring of the plants. If you are near nurseries and other commercial sources, or intend to use wild plants that you collect, you have no problem here. If you are going to send for at least some of your plants, then you should allow an average of two weeks to receive them, depending on the location of the supplier and the type of transport you select. You should place your orders so the plants will be at hand conveniently soon after the terrarium case is ready. If plants arrive too soon, keep them in shade; sink potted plants in your temporary placement box and keep the soil moist; check any plants sent in plastic and embedded in sphagnum moss to see if water is needed.

The second timing point concerns supplies, so that you gradually gather, on shopping trips or country walks, the materials you will need when planting day arrives. You will need pebbles and small stones for drainage—and get more than you think you will need; a small rock or two for the higher ground in your landscape, or as part of a vine and creeping plant corner; and flat pieces of rock for insulating walls underground. These may of course be collected on one trip to the country if you are a city dweller, or they may be purchased.

While you are taking a country trip, visiting garden supply stores, or making out an order for mailing, be sure to include moss. Setting out with a pail, trowel, and sheets of plastic to

put between layers of moss can turn a woods walk into a
treasure hunt. But a time-saving way is to order some of the
interesting varieties of moss by mail. Sheet moss from a
florist is a last resort, as the color when water is added is not
as attractive as that of some other types.

You can buy packages of soil suitable for a terrarium at a
florist's or garden shop. If you want to mix your own, an all-
purpose medium is one third garden soil, one third sharp sand,
one third humus or peat moss. As mentioned in the first chapter, plants which need different types of soil may be set apart
with insulating walls or barriers. The sand should be builders'
sand, or a well-washed equivalent, and can be got from a
contractor as well as a garden store. Many hardware stores
carry peat moss. You will also need a small bag of charcoal.

All during your preparations, the most interesting part continues—choosing the plants. You may want to shop around at
local nurseries to see what a given plant looks like. If so, a
phone call ahead will make sure that the nursery handles
miniature plants or others you might want to inspect. You may
want to send away for certain plants from sources listed at
the back of the book. In any event, having decided what sort
of final effect you want for your terrarium, you set things in
motion to acquire the plants.

To illustrate the possibilities, you might have a tropical terrarium, or a wildlife grouping, or a more general selection,
arranged with points of special interest.

Plants for the tropical effect are in lavish supply. A start
can be made with plants that settle in easily, moving on gradually to those needing more attention. Remember that the
tropical scene need not be literally all tropical plants, but may
include some which need humidity and give the tropical
effect.

There should be one or two small palms, of course. Ferns
are a must, with many to choose from; maidenhair fern is
especially attractive and likes the humidity. For flowers, this
is an opportunity for miniature gesneriads. In the tropical
scene illustrated (Figure 13) I used three gesneriads, two seen
flowering. Miniature begonias thrive in the moist air and have

attractive foliage. Vines and mosses grow lushly here, covering bare spots of soil and spreading green against the glass.

A tropical terrarium can include young plants that have larger leaves and grow readily, to be pruned back as needed, letting the foliage rise in a mass toward the top. Here you will have to decide whether you want ultimately to have a jungle, or a scene with accents of individual plants and arrangements.

A terrarium of plants gathered in the country not only makes an attractive garden, but also has the personal slant of including your own discoveries. Here the selecting depends on the part of the country in which you live. You can experiment, or a nurseryman will advise you on local plants and flowers that will thrive in the humid air of a terrarium.

A special-interest terrarium can be as individual as you like, and gives scope for both intriguing plants and flowers, and overall landscaping. Here are suggestions. Plant most of the taller foliage plants at the back, with plenty of room left in the foreground. At the front use one of two groupings for height contrast, but in the main keep the planting low so separate plants can be seen in detail.

Then for a point of interest, use an arrangement of small rocks, with a vine or creeping plant in the middle spreading out and down; you can use creeping fig (*Ficus pumila*), seen at the left in the waterfall garden, or needlepoint ivy, or the ever-useful *Helxine soleirolii*. Another accent can be a small piece of branch that resembles a miniature log, a bit of driftwood, or a curl of birch bark. Against this, put one or two plants according to size, or a small fern. In Figure 13, I used a miniature bromeliad on a curl of bark, which would fit this scene also. Another point of interest in the foreground can be a pool. Use a small clear glass bowl in a nest of moss, or a pottery bowl in a color that simulates a woodland pool, with a flat rock, moss, or vines across the rim. The pool will contain tiny plants floating on the surface that may be bought at an aquarium store. The pool in Figure 14 has a flat rock at one side, with green-gray lichen growing across it, and at the front I put a clump of British soldier lichen with its tiny red tips.

Select the special-interest arrangement you are going to use, decide its position toward the front of the terrarium, and relate other planting to this, so it is featured quietly. Interesting plants for this terrarium could be a walking fern, which will reach out a frond, touch the soil, and produce a new plant there; a venus flytrap, using an insulating wall to provide marshy ground at a corner; and a small northern pitcher plant in the same corner.

For a more detailed planting at the front, make a winding path of tiny stepping stones that comes out from behind a tall bush, winds its way between plantings of *Sinningia pusilla* or other small gesneriads, passes a tall twig from which hangs a thumb-size basket of vines, and ends at the pool.

You may prefer concentrating on ferns, combining different varieties. Then you might add bromeliads, which offer great interest in both shape and color. Or you may want to try miniature orchids; these may be air-growing, living contentedly in osmunds, and here you might search for a small branch with a good crotch or knothole for osmunda and orchid. Orchids of the terrestrial type can be planted in the soil packaged for African violets, their areas separated as needed by insulating walls underground.

For all three types of terrarium planting, include ground cover so you will have small vines and creepers as well as moss. These are available also from the listed sources.

With your case ready, the list of supplies checked, the plants on hand, planting time has arrived. If your schedule permits, the soil will have been put in place, lightly dampened, and left for a few hours before the start.

First you put in your drainage layer. This is vital in the case without drainage holes, and important also for the second case, as the drainage holes will only be used on the sad occasions when water has been added too liberally. So a layer of pebbles and small stones is put at the bottom, mixed with crushed charcoal. If you can't get charcoal in small enough pieces, break it with a hammer. This layer should be at least an inch deep in the terrarium with the drainage holes, and at least two inches in the other one.

Next the soil goes in, commercial mix or your own. You can

decide whether you want to put an edging of moss, green side out, as a liner against the glass, or if you like the natural effect of earth showing above the bottom of the case.

The soil should be two to three inches deep at the lowest points, depending on the arrangement. Shape hills and slopes, according to your landscaping plan. If the terrarium is to be in the middle of the room occasionally, it can have high ground at the center, with some tall plants there. But since it will be most of the time in front of a window, unless you use fluorescent lighting, it is simpler to make a hill at the back and grade the ground down from there. A good effect is made if the hill is taller at one side, so that even the high ground has a slope of its own.

The planting itself, what to put where, is your individual pleasure. You can follow some of the suggestions given, adapt details from the illustrations, or go your own way. In general, since the terrarium is apt to have three sides with good viewing, the tallest plants are at the back. But this can be varied, if a design is worked out with high ground and taller plants at one side, and the ground falling away in slopes and rockfalls down the other side of the case. Half the fun of making the garden is watching your private and personal design come to life under your fingers.

After you have completed your terrarium and enjoyed it for a while, you may want another for a second room, and this time want to specialize in certain plants that interest you. If you are not experienced in these specific plants, there are organizations, nurserymen, and books from which to get information. Or you may want to combine a terrarium with fluorescent lighting, which offers new possibilities in flowers and also in evening effects.

Though a terrarium needs little care compared to open planters, you should check it frequently for moisture, especially while you work out the amount of time you will leave a vent open at the top for fresh air. This will vary with the time of year and the heating of your home. Inspect the soil, all the way down to the drainage pebbles, to be sure it is damp though not soggy. Though various tools are suggested for this, there is nothing as accurate as your fingers. If the ground is too damp, leave the top off entirely for a few hours, checking as you go. If too dry, water carefully, according to the plants; mist the foliage, except those plants which prefer dry leaves, and close the top for a few hours. Then go back to the usual routine of opening the top an inch or two, either daytime or nightime.

As you get your plants, you will note their preferences on water. But all the planting in a terrarium should benefit from humidity and be chosen accordingly. Too much water could lead to root rotting. So at the start, check more often as you find out how well the terrarium holds moisture and how little water is needed after the start with moist soil.

If you want to try a sealed-top terrarium, then of course it will go without watering, after a properly moist start, for weeks at a time. Begin with a simple one, to see for yourself the effect of condensation on the glass, and to make sure you wouldn't rather have a terrarium with easy regulation of fresh air. Take a glass bowl, plant it with small ferns, tape the glass top on firmly, and watch your experiment.

A terrarium with glass sides and no top will need daily checking for dryness. Again, why not try a small one. There are a lot of miniature flowers living in brandy snifters these days. But also you might look through your glass and crystal, or wander around in shops, to find a container that is different and your own. Plant it with a small fern and a Johnny-jump-up, with moss for a ground cover. Or use the miniature flower you found for yourself as you went through a greenhouse.

You may get interested in experimenting and making a variety of small terrariums for gifts. You may have a row of planted bowls and wine glasses under your fluorescent desk lamp. And you may find yourself drifting through shops with an eye out for glass containers, seeing them not as ornaments or sugar bowls, but as happy homes for your miniature plants.

10. No-Sun Gardens

A GARDEN FOR THE SHADY CORNER OF A ROOM, OR FOR A room with no sunlight, is worked out first of all with a list of plants that will tolerate these conditions. The list can be compiled from visits to nurseries, from suggestions here, or from catalogs. Personal preferences, the character of the room, the size of the planter, and similar factors will determine an individual list, with plants that combine well for a characterful garden.

Rotation of plants is another part of the solution. The list of possible plants is broadened if some of them can be rotated, spending part of the time in another room in sunlight. For this reason, arrangements including pots are more acceptable than usual. In some planters, the pots may be sunk to soil level, as mentioned elsewhere. If they are to be in view, special care in selection is important. Flowerpots have come quite a way from the old-fashioned red clay version.

To get away from a mélange of plants in pots of indiscriminate shape and color, huddled together or strung out before a window, use a basic color for the pots. This depends on the color scheme of the room, of course, but white pots are frequently effective. They should, for the most part, be the same shape but in different sizes. There will be larger pots for larger plants, to place at the rear, or as part of the design, at one side or in balance. Flowerpots that add to the pattern won't look forlorn or happenchance.

A tier of plant shelves, with the shelves preferably of glass to simplify detail and let light through, can hold pots of graded sizes, with a garden in a long planter for the focus. Saucers should match the pots or each other. This plant stand can go in front of a window; it can be used against a dark wall, with rotation of the plants. The planter might stress the many ferns that accept shade.

A triangular table can be made for a corner, to hold potted plants. This simplifies rotation. Otherwise the floor planter described in Chapter 4 can be used, with the plants directly in the soil.

An oblong table set across a corner, with light arranged behind it, combines effect with an assist for the plants. Here again there would be a planter and pots. The light could be trained on the planter, or partly concealed behind foliage.

Most plants benefit from some direct daylight, if not some degree of sunlight, but quite a few of them can make a good adjustment to poor light. Select the ones that are known to need less light, but watch them also. Plants can vary individually. If a plant is not prospering, is starting to look spindly and rather discouraged, take it away to a better light and substitute something else.

Rotation is valuable as an aid to plant health, permits more variety of choice, and allows for a rest period for plants that are dormant part of the year. It also permits the use of plants which lose their foliage seasonally.

In order to rotate plants to better light for an interval, a base is set up in any room with sunlight. If you have a sunny pantry with space at a window, or an extra sunny bedroom, fine; the kitchen is another possibility, especially if the stove is electric rather than gas; when there is limited space, sometimes people will yield a sunny window to the plants, and the work table or desk can be moved out a little way to make space for a plant shelf at windowsill level. The main things are sun and easy access for watering and other care.

In considering rest periods, while most plants have a dormant period, this is more noticeable with some than others. As you note the appropriate culture for plants you select, you can check the matter of a rest period, so a little care here will result in sturdier plants. Variations in temperature, light, and limited watering and feeding during the dormant period are part of the program. You may plan ahead to allow for plants that have a resting period that is longer or occurs at specific seasons. Or you may realize suddenly that a plant which has had a time of active growth, and now no longer is showing new leaves, has reached a rest period. Quite a few foliage plants have short resting periods, or can manage their way through without special care.

On the special list should be plants for the floor planter that gets no sunlight. When the planter is large enough so that tall plants that reach up toward the ceiling will be in proportion, the rubber plant with its long leaves makes a good background choice. This contrasts well with the leaves of the fiddle-leaf fig. Screw-pine gives further variation in foliage; it may profit from a trip to sunlight occasionally. If a Swiss cheese plant is used for sizable effect and because it does well without sun, a plant with smaller leaves or a vine on a support should be combined with it or placed in front of it, to cut down the massive effect. Ivy-arum can be trained on a support for this.

Tough and durable plants for this floor planter are aspidistra and snake plant, which adapt to a dim light, and add to the foliage effect while more interesting plants are featured. *Sansevieria trifasciata*, or snake plant, is all too familiar. *Sansevieria trifasciata hahni*, not quite so well known, is also accommodating.

Aglaonema oblongifolium curtisi, a Chinese evergreen, gives height and likes shade. Norfolk Island pine is an interesting enough addition to repay moving it to sunlight for intervals, if the planter is in poor light.

Along the front of the planter may be an inset panel, a separate container, for peperomia plants with their ornamental foliage. These may accept the position or may need removal to the sun periodically, according to the amount of light in the particular room. There are varying degrees of shaded corners, and the plants will do their own light-metering.

Also along the front can be sansevieria again, this time dwarf variety. Pachysandra often settles into a shaded room corner as comfortably as outdoors under a tree.

If the floor planter is made deep enough to permit it, some of the plants can be left in pots and sunk in the soil, for easier rotation. With this depth, and the resultant taller front rim, vines spreading out over the edge are more important.

A planter recessed to floor level, with good depth, makes an excellent appearance. It will have a rim that suits the room, of metal, whitewashed brick, tile. However this is an extensive project that may not win the vote in a family council meeting.

Vines on a trellis that catches no sunlight needn't be entirely philodendron, useful as that is. There is nephthytis, with rather large leaves. Kangaroo vine is another possibility.

Vines that add distinction to a dull stretch of wall, where something smaller than a trellis is wanted, are grown in their own pot rather than a planter. This can be a large floor pot. Green bamboo stakes are set in the pot for the vines to climb, sometimes with cross pieces wired between them. Nephthytis can be used here; or there is wax vine, with better results when rotated.

A garden in a table planter for a sunless room can at least have daylight close to a window, and many plants thrive there. For this garden, 'Emerald Ripple' (Figure 7), a peperomia, can be featured for its foliage. Some of the gesneriads do well in a north window. Several dwarf palms thrive without sun. Dieffenbachia takes a north window, and sometimes jade plant, though the latter may need a sunning trip occasionally. If the garden is large enough to take height, the Norfolk Island pine can stay in the north window without moving.

The room without sun is a good place for a fern garden. Ferns offer enough contrast to make an effective garden by themselves. Or they may be used as the planting around a miniature waterfall, as described in Chapter 2.

In addition to dwarf ferns, young specimens of larger varieties may be used and later transplanted, moving to the floor planter or elsewhere when they get too large for the window garden. While shopping at a greenhouse, ask for young ferns, which may not always be in sight. Also keep a lookout for them, among larger plants. After being told there were no small ferns available at a greenhouse, I found exactly the right kind in a forgotten corner. Ferns may be ordered by mail, and they travel well except in extreme weather. Among the ferns for the no-sun window are bird's nest, holly fern, ball fern, table fern, silver lace.

House trees give an individual touch to the sunless room, in their own large pots, or planted in a floor garden. Rotation makes it possible to have flowering trees on occasion. You may prefer real trees, potted appropriately, for example a palm in a bamboo floor pot with a metal liner. Or you may want trees you have shaped yourself, by pruning and training them against strong stakes, till you have a rose tree, a geranium tree. Or again, you may grow your own avocado tree.

Ivy trees, mentioned earlier, can be stylized formally, or the ivy can be trained over wire shapes into unusual designs. Ivy can also be trained to cover wire mesh shaped like a small columned tree and filled with sphagnum moss, which is kept moist, and there the ivy will eventually take hold. Ivy, often taken for granted, should have sun on occasion and should have regular watering and misting.

Getting back to real trees again, of smaller variety, gardens with miniature trees can stay in this room with rotation. The culture of bonsai is discussed in another chapter. But dwarf and miniature trees, taken as they are with perhaps a little pruning, can play an important part in indoor gardens. Select those that take indoor life, don't give them too much heat, and mist them as well as water them.

Since a good compromise can be worked out for the sunless room, with some plants staying in the room and some rotated, further programming can be added. Plants that are in pots buried rim-deep in soil can shelter there for the winter in cold climates, and be moved to patio or porch in the summer. A special corner of the patio can be prepared, with a concrete planter sunk into the ground. The porch can have a floor planter, or a wide bench in a sheltered place.

In the South, green foliage makes a cool linking of rooms with patio, done with room dividers or simply with the matching pattern of leaves on both sides of glass sliding doors. Local plants often transfer easily indoors, and many tropical plants feel at home there, without sudden cold drafts and massive steam heating, the choice again depending on the no-sun list, or on rotation. In a South Florida patio we had two floor planters, one in the sun and one not, and used about two-thirds no-sun plants in the shaded garden, moving the other third to the sunny garden one at a time. At the back of the shaded garden were several tough and good-natured plants that were moved about to fill any gap caused by rotation.

Crotons should be considered when there is a large enough sunny base for rotation. They won't do happily without any sun, but are worth the trouble of transporting, with foliage of a surprising color range, often in combination, such as leaves that combine yellow and red, and others varying from pink to orange to red.

Since the room without sun is a location where pots may be more in evidence, a tray with sufficiently high sides for pebbles and water will ensure that though the plants won't find sunlight they will have some humidity. As with the plant stand, carefully selected and placed pots will provide a design instead of a clutter.

A container for small plants, some flowering, helps easy transfer to sunlight if the planter is filled with peat moss. This can be easily tested to make sure it is kept moist, and the pots moved in and out readily. Clay pots should be used rather than plastic.

For a number of similar pots to be grouped together on a table or broad shelf, solid glass blocks or other matching units provide different levels for the plants, and build an unusual

Figure 16

Ira Finke

A gesneriad, Sinningia *'Dollbaby' is in flower at the center. At the left and front is seen a walking fern, which eventually moved to wider walking space in the waterfall garden.*

design. Here again, the unity of the glass blocks, and careful planning, will turn a collection of separate items into a related garden effect.

Interesting plants in a brandy snifter can flower in sunlight and then move to the coffee table in a sunless room (Figure 16). The glass sides provide some humidity for plants needing it.

Among the plants that tolerate little or no sun better than most is the *Cyperus alternifolius*, sometimes called the umbrella palm. This grows tall so should be placed accordingly. A small relative of the rubber plant, *Ficus pumila* or creeping fig, often grows well without sun. Coleus is bright and takes shade, but grows with abandon and must be watched for pests. Also adaptable to shade but susceptible to the same mealybugs is the pick-a-back plant, or piggy-back plant, a saxifrage, which sends out new small plants from its older leaves, at the point where the leaves join the stalk. This is a diverting plant for a small accent.

Some of the bromeliads that grow in shade should be considered while you shop for plants. In addition to flowers, they have foliage of interesting shape and color. Some grow in soil, some in osmunda. They can be used for individual effect in small planters, or placed near the front of a larger planter.

With a sunless room and a busy program, instead of much rotation, plants that prefer shade or accept it should be used. But with time to spend on growing plants in the sun, and then transferring them for a while to the sunless room, specialization gives added interest.

For example, concentrate on geraniums. They have come a long way from the spradling plants on a kitchen shelf, the motif of red pots of red geraniums in a row of cottage windows.

Varieties of geraniums run into the hundreds, regular size, dwarf, and miniature. A garden of miniatures can be planned with formal rows or banked plants.

The African violet or *Saintpaulia*, a widely known gesneriad, can be grown and will flower in a north window, but does better in moderate sun. It can spend long visits in the sunless room. New varieties of African violets are constantly being added to suppliers' plant lists. They repay pains with watering, humidity, protection from gas; however, they need not be watched for a resting period. Other gesneriads offer more unusual effects, as discussed later.

Philodendron cordatum should be included somewhere in the sunless room, in a hanging basket, climbing a trellis, trailing across the edge of a planter. It will grow in a dim corner for longer than many plants, but responds better when it is near daylight.

To cut down the amount of rotation and permit more choice of plants, fluorescent lighting should be considered. It can be used for a single planter, or more widely. A lamp or a wall fitting with incandescent bulbs, though of course not equivalent to fluorescent lighting, is gratefully received by many plants.

The planter with its own lights, as described in Chapter 3, encourages plant growth. Any combination of a lamp and a garden that suits the room helps compensate for no sun.

11. Seasonal Gardens

SEASONS ARE REFLECTED IN INDOOR GARDENS, NOT ONLY BY changes that fit the time of year, but also by preparations for the season to follow. Plants in a window container may display attractive foliage, while they are on their way toward bloom next season.

For anyone living in a climate with strongly defined seasons, planning ahead is important. The outdoor gardeners are used to this. Indoor gardening benefits too, especially for apartment dwellers.

Each of the four seasons will have plants to stress then. Each has projects for that time of year.

A late spring or a cold spring may be hesitating outside the windows, but inside at least one planter can mark the calendar correctly. Daffodils and tulips in bloom, large or miniature, can look through the panes at the last snow flurry.

Primroses belong in a spring planter, flowering in many colors. They need a cool temperature and good humidity, and benefit as the thermostat is set lower.

If you planned ahead you will have your own flowers for Easter. That means planning quite a bit ahead for lilies, but there are quantities of other flowers to work with more quickly for Easter time.

For a small movable garden to use on the breakfast table and start the day with a springlike air, grape hyacinths make a good showing. The planter should stay in a cool room for most of the time.

If someone gives you a potted azalea, no matter how attractively in bloom, stop to consider all the other azaleas sitting tiresomely in their everyday pots or pots covered with foil, and provide something better. You may not have space for it in a deep planter, but with a little shopping around you can find a container that suits the azalea and the room, in pottery or in wood with a metal liner.

Spring should be the climax for the seeds planted during the winter. Your seedlings will have emerged long since from their first dimly lighted stage, progressing on to sunlight, and now should be convinced that regardless of the outside thermometer it's time to bloom. Some plants insist on their own season of blooming, in spite of being given a head start, but many will change their habits.

In an apartment, the season should be marked with special spring gardens. There are no leaves to rake, no late frost to worry about. These are gardens for personal choices, for flowers that meant the end of winter to you as a child, or colors that will bring the country to your window. If time is limited, plants can be bought already in bud. You can take vines from another planter or from your base supply, so the new flowering plants will fit among the green and look at home quickly. Of all the seasons, this is the time to disregard color schemes for once, and let the colors mix as if the wind planted the flowers.

Spring is also an ordering time for the wildlife garden. Plants for this garden are in best supply during spring and fall, and some suppliers only ship them then or do so in other seasons at the customer's risk. A wildlife garden started in the spring has the added advantage of warm months ahead in which you can search for plants yourself through the countryside, as well as for rocks, curls of bark, and moss.

A wildlife planter for the apartment can progress slowly in landscaping, as country trips add new material. Also on these trips, extra rocks, small bits of branches for miniature logs, twigs for fences, and other interesting items can be collected and stored in a box at the back of a closet, ready for wintertime planters later on.

And sometime during this season, plants can be brought along in good shape for summer blooming. Fuchsias, for example, in a relatively cool room, repay spring attention with a variety of summer flowers.

During summer, the merging of indoors and outdoors is added to by planters. Flowering plants from garden beds outdoors move in to the planters. Some of the plants that have spent their time inside now go to the garden for a season, usually still in their pots to be sunk to rim level.

The merging of indoors and outdoors can be emphasized, in city or country, by a combination of window box and large planter, on the two sides of the same window. This is effective whether the window is open, closed, or screened.

The planter should be at windowsill level, matching the position of the outside box. The two are planted identically with flowering plants, so they seem one large garden. Foliage plants may be taller at the ends of the window box to provide a framing effect. But the main emphasis is on a garden that seems to continue across the windowsill. With a little care when the window is closed or the screen put in, branching flowers can be allowed to reach across the space.

For a room with north or east light, fuchsias and tuberous begonias are a good choice. Small planters with miniatures still have their place, but adding a large, deep planter gives scope for taller summer flowers.

Adding greenery to a room for its cool look may be done with plans to convert the container later. A large planter filled with no-sun plants, set on a low table or wide stool near a summer grouping of furniture or on the porch, may be used in the winter as a floor planter in a corner needing brightening. Tubs or large redwood pots in the same way give foliage plants an outside season on the terrace or steps, planned for indoor use in specific positions later.

Color may be chosen to blend with the room, in flowers for a sunny window planter. Or there can be a selection of cool colors, perhaps white and blue. Blue mist, an appropriate popular name for *Ageratum,* blooms steadily, and seeds planted in early spring indoors will have produced flowering plants now.

Portulacas provide a gay window garden. Sun is a must, as the flowers won't open without it. They can be massed together in a long container, or grouped in several small planters.

A cool effect for summer is a planter that is largely pool. The inset container that will be the pool can be adapted for the purpose, using a pottery bowl in brown or dark blue or green, or glass that sets in a nest of sand and green moss. In the border of soil between edges of the planter and the pool, put small ferns and vines. In the pool itself, use a water hyacinth, or plants you select at an aquarium store. Choice of plants will depend on the size of the pool, especially its depth. Some plants will need pebbles or sand or soil at the bottom, others float on the surface.

Moss baskets and fern balls are an addition to a shaded patio, or on a porch over a planter with contents that can use a drip of water from above. Except in warm climates, the hanging basket will have to be repotted or placed in an outer container for winter use, and the fern ball hung in a carefully planned place indoors.

A simpler hanging basket is described in Chapter 4. The one illustrated in Figure 17 contains a graceful vine, a gesneriad, *Hypocyrta wettsteinii,* and a small begonia, both flowering.

Summer is the time to start a planted branch for the wintertime room wall. This is described in Chapter 13. To find an attractive branch, several woods walks may be needed.

Marigolds and nasturtiums make a bright window garden for an apartment. Dwarf pinks can make a border against a mass of white alyssum.

At odd times during the summer, seeds and cuttings can be started, to be ready for their use in fall planters. Chrysanthemums should be selected for the size and color that will best suit a room and container in the fall.

Vines can get a head start now, for later use. If some of the

Figure 17

Ted Budlong

Hypocyrta wettsteinii *trails its glossy leaves and bright flowers, with a small begonia showing near the chains, in a ceramic hanging basket, its color chosen to blend with the wood behind it.*

vines are planted in crystal bowls lined with moss, they make attractive additions to a room, while they are waiting to be used in future gardens (Figure 18).

It may be harder for those with outside gardens distracting them to plan ahead for room planters. But there is the advantage of space, so plants of garden borders, spreading through the summer, will provide small plants for later indoor use, and there is room for indoor plants to have their stay in the open air. A procession of green moves in and out of the house.

Turning indoors more definitely in the fall, planters are freshened with new planting, and perhaps an added one is being started. This also is a time for repotting.

Some plants will move indoors, comfortable in the same pots, to be sunk again in floor planters. Others have outgrown their pots and need the next larger size. Plants that have been directly in the soil in garden beds may need roots trimmed before they are put in a planter again. A plant may have outgrown its original planter, flourishing in summer open air, and now have a large floor planter. Two or three of the more sizable plants, in wooden floor pots with liners that have been made with a specific room in mind, can have a gracious garden look, arranged together. If plants are transferred from garden soil to pots, they do well with a week of outside air before going indoors. When possible, one change at a time—of transplanting, temperature, light—is a good general rule.

Some gardeners prefer to repot in late spring or early summer. But in any case, there will be changes needed by fall. If a plant should not have its roots trimmed, but has produced what seems an alarming amount of roots, don't be tempted to put it in a much larger pot. The next size larger, step by step, is a time-honored rule. When you want to use a plant in a large floor tub for the effect of the container, sink the pot again, while the plant grows. If you are combining it with a taller plant, the size of the container should be planned to accommodate both plants with one in a pot.

For those living in apartments, there are problems with plants needing summer care, fall care. For these special plants, such as azaleas, a visit away from home is indicated. This may mean taking the plants to a garden-minded friend in the country. Or plants may be boarded out at a greenhouse, to get the right summer conditions and care and a good start for the fall return.

Garden plants for indoor use must of course be brought in well before frost. It is a good idea to have a few extra emergency plants, of the kind needed for a specific indoor garden; these can be waiting in a pot, for replacements, in case one or two plants in the container don't respond well to the move.

The chrysanthemum planter offers a glowing fall array. If the planter is large enough, the plants may have been potted during the summer and sunk into beds, so the move indoors will be simplified, and once again the pots will be sunk into the planter soil. Flowers should last through fall into winter.

A fall arrangement for sideboard or table can combine one or two plants with leaves and fruit, in vivid colors. In Figure 24 I used a *Sinningia speciosa* in a large bowl of dark green glass, with peaches from trees outside the windows, and a spray of dogwood.

Some fall time should be given to starting the bulb program. You probably have your own schedule for bulbs, whether you use a cold frame at the start or a cool indoor location, or purchase bulbs that already have had a cool period. If you are using some varieties of bulbs that you're not familiar with, of course you will check the timing for the sequence of development, the timing before bloom may be expected, and begin accordingly. The proper fall start furnishes blooms in winter and spring.

Some bulbous plants started in the fall produce flowers by December, others in March and April. For quick results, crocuses will provide a small garden in a few weeks. Fall crocus bulbs are used for this. If you postpone using them, check the bulbs regularly to make sure they aren't developing and so need planting at once.

Bulbs have a natural place in apartment life. But don't stop with varieties of narcissus. Try freesia for a taller garden, with stakes and green garden twine as they grow. Or investigate miniature bulbs. These can be started in September in a cool, dark corner, to move later to the light. They will need a cool windowsill.

Fall ordering for the wildlife planter should be done in good time. Orders can include plants that will be useful on hand later, such as partridge-berry in December. This is also a good time to order plants for children's gardens, which are discussed in detail in Chapter 14.

Figure 18

Ira Finke

Vines waiting to be planted in an indoor garden can make their own simple effect in crystal bowls. Pilea depressa *grows in the larger bowl,* Helxine soleirolii *in the other.*

In addition to planning and planting for the future, fall sees the indoor gardens ready for the colder months. They will have fresh soil as needed, plants will be pruned, and any that have grown unevenly, throwing out the garden design of the planter, can be shifted to a new position or exchanged for another plant.

In the winter, indoor gardens have their most dramatic period, contrasting to the weather outside. You may want a large planter of bright tall flowers, such as bird-of-paradise.

You may choose small callas, or dwarf marigolds that you grew from seeds.

If among your bulbs you planted miniatures, you can have a garden of them blooming in winter, with larger varieties planned for spring. A garden with only tiny tulips in different colors will sometimes be more effective than a mixture of flowers.

As Christmas approaches, a snowy afternoon can be spent preparing the berry bowls, described in Chapter 13, and the Christmas garden mentioned in Chapter 6. With an assist from fluorescent lighting, red flowers may be timed for the holidays.

Winter is a good time to get acquainted with new varieties of miniatures, in movable gardens. Winter may also provide time for specialization.

Bromeliads, originally from the tropics, offer much interest for specialization and are rewarding for winter gardens, with unusual foliage and flowers. As mentioned earlier, they make excellent accents for a design. Or you may decide that a definitely marked plant, such as the zebra plant, deserves a small planter to itself. Bromeliads are not difficult to care for, and adapt well to apartment living.

In southern climates, tropical flowers are part of the daily scene, but they add a vivid indoor touch to northern winters. Some are so familiar we may have accepted them as house plants without considering their origin; others can introduce a new combination of shape and color. The gesneriads, also of tropical origin, like the bromeliads have a wide and interesting variety, and are a rewarding choice for specialization.

If winter stays too long, a garden that looks toward spring can be filled with lily of the valley, home-grown. Frozen pips can be purchased ready for speedy growth, with bloom in less than a month.

Seeds should be planted during winter, for your own Easter flowers and spring gardens. Get a seed catalog, dream a little, plant a little, and spring will be almost with you.

12. Personalized Gardens

MOST INDOOR GARDENS SHOW AN INDIVIDUAL TOUCH. THIS IS EM-
phasized, with unusual gardens as a result, when they are
planned around a special personal interest.

Travel can provide a garden in which each plant represents
a trip. At the start, the planter would have a background of
foliage plants, with the new additions taking the spotlight in
front; gradually trip plants replace the original background.
Also at the start, short trips would produce cuttings and plants,
which would give way later to plants from faraway places.

A travel case for the plants is a help in easy transport. It
could be an old camera case on a shoulder strap, lined with
plastic, or a waterproof box that has been given a handle. A
small strap fastened inside makes a secure rest for a miniature
watering pot, and sphagnum moss should be included for holding moisture and for packing around a plant to keep it in
place.

An inside and outside garden can be used together for plants
from trips. We collected rose slips once, each marking a
special garden in a special place. These grew indoors, under
glass jars for the terrarium effect of humidity, the jars being

removed regularly and briefly for watering and fresh air. As
the rose plants grew and the outdoor season arrived, some of
the taller roses moved to an outdoor bed and new slips took
their places.

In collecting plants to mark trips, when there is any question of restrictions on transport into the country or across a
state line, there are solutions. A plant can be selected from
a supplier who is set up to ship in conformity with regulations;
the selecting supplies the personal angle, and the plant can
reach you soon after you return. Or you can use seeds, which
you will sow yourself.

A very personal garden, to progress as rapidly or slowly as
desired, can be centered around plants identified with special
occasions. This association garden can have a dry humor just
as easily as it can be sentimental.

A garden can also catch the quality of a single place seen
on a trip. This can be a tropical island, an English garden, a
desert scene. A feature of the place that has individualized
interest can be stressed.

Here is another exception to the general rule of not using
decorations such as tiny plaster gnomes, toadstools, and other
bric-à-brac in the gardens. When you build a garden that is
identified with a specific place, the small scene can reproduce
in miniature some of the original features. A formal garden is
keyed to its larger original, for example, by a small copy of the
arched trellis for vines with a seat under it.

You may go further with this, in reproducing part of a home
garden, or a garden remembered from childhood. The miniature home garden, for instance, could be planned to duplicate
a carefully chosen corner of your yard, with a fence or wall
corner that can be modeled easily small-scale, and the same
plants if they can be used indoors readily, otherwise plants
that give the same general effect in miniature.

A family project, complicated but rewarding, would be a
small replica of your house and garden. But it's easier to select
some characteristic part of the outdoor garden—such as the
tool shed covered with vines, the rock garden, the gate with
a large plant in a tub on each side, the stepping-stone path

with beds beside it, the pool with water dripping down from a concealed source among rocks—and copy this for an indoor garden. An easy way to get a dramatic copy is to choose a new effect for the outdoor garden, planning it for future reproduction in miniature. This can be a new small waterfall for the outdoor pool, to be copied in the waterfall indoor garden of Chapter 2, each with the same design; or a brick path between flower beds near a tree, outside, that can be reproduced indoors with tiny beds, bits of brick, and a miniature tree.

Personalized gardens may take longer in the making than other indoor gardens, but their progress is interesting. And a partial temporary planting can be used, meanwhile.

Sometimes you may plan an indoor garden for a long time, deciding the details, locating places to get the plants that will be needed, searching for just the right planter, before you finally start it. You might modify your original plan, according to the climate where you live, whether it is an apartment or a house, how much sunny space you have. And you would probably find, en route, plants that fit the plan effectively that you hadn't thought of at first.

Anticipation and planning add their bit to the satisfaction when the garden is finally finished. So a mental gallery of gardens ahead to be attained has its own pleasures.

In this way I have sometimes planned indoor gardens, that were not made for years till a move to a different climate, or the exact right house, fitted the particular garden. One indoor garden has interested me for some time, and is still to be completed. Details follow, for someone else who might be interested.

This is a garden that would be composed entirely of plants and flowers that have their origin in legend and myth, herbs used in early days for curative effects as well as witchcraft, plants that were once believed to have magical powers. A garden of legends, with a story for each plant.

I have collected quite a list of plants for this garden, some of which will be mentioned here. Of these, some will grow readily indoors, some are still to be checked for special needs and an amiable size.

Anyone starting this garden would have an individual list of plants, also, depending on special interests. And reading will result in further ideas for plants. The English poets, as far back as Chaucer, mentioned plants believed to have special powers, special uses. Shakespeare provides plants for fairies as well as witches. When you come across a copy of *Dracula*, you will notice garlic and wild rose used as a protection against vampires and werewolves. Frazer's *Golden Bough* is a must for this type of reading. Any of the early herbals, with their stress on plants having magic uses, will provide ideas. Culpeper's *English Physician and Complete Herball* is rewarding, and there is an arrangement of this for use as a first-aid herbal by Mrs. C. F. Leyel. Other books suggested are Joseph Wood Krutch's *The Gardener's World; A Witch's Guide to Gardening* by Dorothy Jacob; and *Green Enchantment* by Rosetta E. Clarkson. The language of flowers is an old tradition that can have a place here. A special division of plants could include those with legendary features in their names, such as dragonroot and fairy fans.

Some plants must have a traditional use that is still to be discovered, and there are waiting empty places on my list. Everyone knows that the way to catch a unicorn is while it is asleep with its head in a virgin's lap. But before catching the unicorn, it has to be found, and in some old book there must be a plant mentioned that will help us locate a unicorn.

When you have a legend garden, be sure to hang mistletoe near it at Christmas time. Mistletoe has a long and magical history. It was used as a cure for epilepsy and as a general healer, and was also sacred to the Druids. In Frazer it is mentioned, as well as rowen and woodbine, as protection against witchcraft. Mistletoe, the golden bough itself, is part of the myths and superstitions of many countries.

Woodbine, a variety of honeysuckle, can be a charm against witches for the garden. After coaxing honeysuckle indoors, it then may need to be firmly restrained.

Monkshood, a common name for *Aconitum,* is a perennial herb that was once believed to be a poison for witches. Nowadays the drug aconite is derived from *A. napellus.* This herb was also called wolfsbane, being used to poison arrows used in hunting wolves.

It is generally know that digitalis, used as a heart stimulant, is derived from foxglove, *Digitalis purpurea.* But elecampane, or *Inula helenium,* known as a hardy foliage herb, is less often recognized as a source of insulin; elecampane was used by early Greeks and Romans as a medicine, and was held to be under the dominion of Mercury.

If plants as tall as elecampane are used, a floor planter might be considered. Or there could be a combination of floor garden and a smaller garden in a movable planter close by.

Trollius is a small perennial herb. As its name indicates, it was once believed to belong to the trolls. A tall herb, dock, was believed useful in breaking the spell of a fairy. Ragwort was important to leprechauns. Wild thyme had its associations with fairies. And to be included among plants with names that suit the garden, there are dragonhead, a herb of the mint family; leopard's-bane, a small variety of perennial herb; fairy wand, a perennial herb; and a lily, fairy bells.

Some of the plants mentioned as herbs are commonly considered weeds nowadays. But they would have been carefully tended in the herb garden of any self-respecting witch.

Flowers have an important place in the legend garden. In addition to flowering plants already mentioned, these include:

Portulaca, once believed to have curative powers

Marigolds, useful in witchcraft as well as early herbal medicine

Lily of the valley, with a reputation for improving a weak memory

Violets, used as poultices for inflammation

Heliotrope, considered good for both gout and warts

Periwinkle, under the dominion of Venus, suggested for man and wife to vitalize their love

The primrose, which once belonged to the fairies

The Christmas rose, *Helleborus niger,* a perennial herb with flowers resembling wild roses, believed to be a charm used by witches

In collecting plants that have been used in past times for curative purposes, it could be interesting to choose those ones dating back to periods when most medicines were derived from plants, which are used for the same purposes today in herbal treatment and in modern medicine. Other ancient plant remedies go into the division of cures for past use only, such as wormwood, a perennial herb, once considered a good remedy for the bite of a sea serpent. Wormwood, or *Artemisia,* has another point of interest: *A. absinthium* is used in the making of absinthe.

There need be no lack of variety in the garden. A dwarf holly can belong there, for the early magical properties of holly, such as protection from lightning and witches, and also as a remedy for colic. Beans were an important part of early rituals and fertility rites, so a scarlet runner bean could be included. Garlic should be planted somewhere in the garden, in case of vampires.

Some of the less familiar plants belong in the garden by old tradition. Costmary or alecost was a herb used to flavor beer. The European pennyroyal, a mint, was used for a cooling drink. Angelica, a tall herb, was once held to have angelic healing powers, and also to be useful as a charm against evil spirits. Sweet cicely, a herb with leaves used in cooking, also provided seeds to make an old-time oil for floor polishing. And a perennial, meadowsweet, was once a sacred plant of the Druids.

More familiar plants include:

Dill, used by magicians for spells, and incidentally also as a charm against their spells

Milfoil, or yarrow, with a legendary history of being used by Achilles to stop bleeding wounds

Pinks, once used for a cordial, as a strengthener

Coriander, considered an aid in calling up devils

Saint-John's-wort, a small herb, known as a fairy horse, responsible for carrying people away at night

Rosemary, used to break magic spells as well as for remembrance

Mignonette, called a magic herb by early Romans

Anise, with seeds expected to avert the evil eye

The mints go far back. The botanical name, *Mentha,* was taken from the name of a nymph who caught the interest of Pluto. In the Bible, mint was used for a tithe. It has been used as a strewing herb, as a fragrance after the bath in ancient Greece, and according to Pliny was useful in keeping mentally alert. Its uses for food and drink have been as numerous as its varieties.

A garden might be centered on herbs that would have been found in a monastery garden in the Dark Ages, when the knowledge of curative herbs and other useful plants was preserved there—which incidentally accounts for the Latin and Greek turn of so many botanical names.

Returning to the fairies, elves, and witches of an earlier day, it can be noted that one of the several names for foxglove was witches' thimbles. Some of the herbs used for witches' spells had to be gathered at the correct phase of the moon. Herbs used to counteract witches' spells also had to be gathered at suitable times. Herbs for witches' spells were often used in combination, frequently seven or nine of them. A recipe to guard against nocturnal goblin visitors listed fourteen herbs.

Plants of our own early times, though less ancient, have their interest. For example, in colonial days, one of the chrysanthemums, *C. balsamite,* the costmary mentioned earlier, was taken to church as a fragrant prayer-book or Bible marker, and was called bible leaf.

These plants are only a few of those with legendary history, strange early use, curative use at a time when medical practice relied strongly on herbal lore, and the many plants whose use was intertwined with primitive religions, ancient rituals and belief in strange creatures. Plants for a garden of legends can be chosen from among them, whether the legends occasionally have come true or not. The link for them all is a belief in their effective use, held by people of long-ago times. Plants for the garden could concentrate on one division of these early beliefs, or have a mixture according to one's personal fancy. After all, this is a personalized garden, and with so many plants to choose from, no two gardens could be alike.

Herbs are in the majority here. And a few suggestions are

added to those in Chapter 7, or stressed again, for planning and care of the garden. Sun is important. A floor planter for tall herbs should have fluorescent light, if it doesn't get direct sunlight. There are quantities of herbs with interesting histories, small enough so a floor planter isn't necessary. But still there should be a sunny window.

In the winter, there should be fresh air in the room daily—though not from the window next to the plants. Humidity is important as always, and not too high a setting for the thermostat.

Since humidity and cooler rooms are considered by some to lessen the number of winter colds, why not try this, with the legend garden for an excuse. If the family colds improve, the garden can be credited with either a cure or a new legend.

The planter for the garden should be deep enough to provide plenty of root room. General-purpose soil can make a base, with insulating material setting apart plants that need more sand or more leaf mold.

Along with each plant chosen for the garden should go its story. And each story may snowball, as more information is found. Thyme, for example, had many histories in many countries.

If you start being interested in a legend garden, then as usually happens when the subconscious mind makes a note, you'll probably find plants with mythical properties mentioned in the most unlikely books and articles. And when you travel, you'll find plants with local legends that may not be in any book, and with legends that finally came true.

Nicole Maxwell made a thorough job of this. She went in search of plants that had curative properties that seemed legendary, among head-hunters along the Amazon. She brought back plants with new and proved medicinal benefits, as told in her book, *Witch Doctor's Apprentice.*

Obviously the plants chosen for a legend garden, when there are young children in the house, would be checked to make sure that they are as harmless as the next ordinary house plant, when nibbled experimentally. But a glance at the plants mentioned will show a variety of culinary herbs that have a magical history.

A garden with young people in mind could concentrate on flowers that have been used in past times as food. Candied violets—candied rose leaves—candied nasturtiums. Also syrup of violets, marigolds, and clove pinks, for older-time desserts. Nasturtium buds were also pickled. Rose hip jelly—a pleasant older way to take vitamin C. Marigold flowers in broth. Preserved sage flowers. Primrose flowers in salads. Some of these could well be removed from the days-of-old period, and used now, on the table as well as in the garden. It takes a long walk nowadays to locate a candied violet.

Whether the garden is based on fact or myth, a look over the shoulder at older times produces plants that have a colorful history. It's a personal choice, wherever one's interest lies; the variety of herbs with histories is wide enough. And there is always that plant to find which will show the way to a unicorn.

13. Garden Projects

INDOOR GARDENS, IN ADDITION TO THEIR OWN ATTRACTIONS, LEND themselves to a variety of projects. There are also gardens so specialized that the making of them has the detailed program of a project.

Planning a garden for a gift, with a little extra time, has individual returns. When planter and contents are chosen with the person for whom it is intended, and the room where it will stand, clearly in mind, this will be a garden with personality.

This means not merely a general character, in result, such as a casual garden or a formal garden. It should highlight, for example, some plant that is a favorite, or combine flowers of two colors that belong in a particular room.

Covered glass bowls, or small open-top terrariums, make a refreshing change as a gift for someone in hospital. These need no attention, take little space, may stay on a bedside table, and are a pleasant diversion. They may be planted with anything interesting from the home supply of plants or from a nursery. A small flowering plant provides continuing interest.

For a convalescent with too much dragging time, the gift

of all the elements for a small movable planter, ready to complete a garden, provides an easy project and something to brighten the program. The container should have pebbles and soil in place. Plants settled in damp sphagnum moss wrapped in plastic will travel in a large flat box that can be used as a working base, with one side cut free at the corners and temporarily fastened with scotch tape so it can be let down easily. Vines and moss are included. One plant should be unusual enough for a conversation piece.

Planning and planting the garden will only be the beginning. For the convalescent, as plants take hold, grow, and flower, there is progressive interest. Gifts on later visits fit the picture, and can be anything from a tiny watering pot to a plant needed for the garden design.

Children especially can use a new interest during convalescence. For a boy, the swamp garden described in Chapter 14 is accompanied by an active small turtle and turtle food.

A miniature garden room for a little girl who is convalescing forms a double project: first the preparation by the giver, and second the care of tiny plants by the child. Plants in very small containers need to be watered with an eyedropper several times daily, which will help the hours pass.

To start the preparation, as a background to give the impression of a room, a three-walled effect can be made by cutting down a cardboard box or bending cardboard, reinforcing it at the corners so it will stand firmly. This can be covered on the inside with Con-Tact paper, in a small wallpaper pattern.

Toy furniture is collected with the focus on a garden look. There can be diminutive planters in their own small stands, tables to hold long planters, tier tables and coffee tables for plants in bowls. Containers can be purchased—dollhouse china and ornaments that will hold plants. Or they may be improvised from things around the house such as bottle lids, or fashioned from heavy foil. Floor pots and floor planters are easily contrived; prowl the house with a lookout for small-sized containers, and you'll see a plastic pill bottle that can be cut down for a floor tub, a metal box that contained small

candies or cough drops and that sprayed with green paint
will turn into a floor planter. Small match boxes are useful,
painted on the outside and lined with plastic on the inside.

The containers used as examples (Figure 20) include
dollhouse equipment and a toothpaste tube cap. The furniture
has garden-look uses. But a more elaborate room, of course,
can be made by adding further furniture. A row of the planters
in their stands could be used as a room divider.

In planting the containers, the main aims should be variety
in effect and durability for easy care. Plants needing more at-

Figure 19
Ted Budlong

*The branch garden with air plants, discussed in the next chapter, can be
personalized in both construction and planting. The branch illustrated has
a tree section with a large knothole, attached across the fork. The staghorn fern with its unusual fronds takes first place in interest. The other
plants are all bromeliads. From the knothole,* Tillandsia tenuifolia *sprays
out widely; it is seen again at the left end of the branch. A dried seed
pod extends from the knothole, its shape repeating the lines of the fork.
T. recurvata is on the slanting end of the branch under the furthest staghorn curve. T. cincinnata grows straight up on the top of the branch beyond the seed pod. T. ionantha leans out from the front of the branch.*

tention can be included for an older child. The large planters should be completed several days ahead, so the plants are flourishing and any disgruntled plant has been removed. These will need only a daily watering. Seedlings you get from under a tree give the look of tall house plants. *Helxine soleirolii* should be planted with long enough trailers to drip down vine-like from the planters. For the smallest containers, there are two suggestions: have a trial run ahead of time, when you see which plants do well with a limited amount of soil, or of sphagnum moss and nutrient; finally plant specimens of these sturdy varieties on the day the gift is made, so you won't be pinned to a long program of frequent watering, yourself. Don't overlook clover and tiny grasses, for the smallest containers. Start a new trend in miniature weeds; they can look charming and also be tough.

When the gift is ready, be sure to take along some extra sphagnum moss and a pair of tweezers, for mooring a plant loosened in transit. And don't forget the eyedropper and a bottle for water.

Indoor gardens make attractive seasonal gifts. These can be small movable planters, with several done at once for efficiency, using variation in the designs. Hanging baskets, discussed in Chapter 4, are a pleasant change from the gift of a potted plant at Easter time. Berry bowls for Christmas can be made with personal detail work that removes them from the category of the commercial partridge-berry bowl. Small plants with which to make individualized berry bowls can be ordered by mail; and the small terrarium containers (round covered bowls and the traditional glass apples and pears) can also be purchased for planting.

Making a bottle garden, for yourself or for a gift, is a project that provides an interesting small garden that needs no care. You may want to use a wide-mouthed bottle for the first one, such as an apothecary jar, so the planting is easier. But the main things that are needed for any type of bottle garden are an accumulation of special tools, and patience.

Tools, so-called, must be long and slim. These can be made or adapted from something out of the kitchen drawer. They should cover three needs: making a hole in the soil for planting, setting the plant in place, and firming or tamping down the soil around a plant. Any long contrivance with a spade-like end that will pass through the bottle neck will serve to make holes for the plants; look over kindling wood or bits of wooden crate, and make a slender spade. Or the kitchen drawer may provide a slim long-handled spoon you've been using for digging in relish bottles. You can contrive a tool with which to firm earth around a plant from anything that provides a flat surface at the end, such as a very small spool fitted on a stick. Something to transfer the plant into the bottle, and hold it in place while soil is settled around it, is the third need. Long tongs have been suggested. I have used a long-handled, two-pronged fork intended for spearing pickles out of jars. The plant is fitted into the crotch of this fork, braced there lightly by a long stick held in the other hand. The plant can then be lowered into the bottle and its hole in the soil; rest between the prongs while the stick is used to draw soil over the roots; be set accurately without bruising.

The bottle should start thoroughly cleaned. But if you have been disturbed by warnings not to get soil on the inner sides of the bottle in the course of events, relax. A miniature window cleaning job can be done at the end, with damp tissue or cloth made into a swab on a stick, to be followed by polishing with a dry swab.

The usual layer of drainage pebbles and crushed charcoal, at least an inch deep, goes in first. Then use some of your purchased all-purpose soil, that is sifted and sterilized, pouring it in through a piece of stiff paper twisted funnel-wise, at least two inches deep, and deeper for a larger bottle. The soil can be lightly damp before it is put in, or dampened carefully after it is in place, turning it over with the spade and making sure after a few hours that it is generally moist but not too wet for easy planting.

Ferns are a good starter for the first bottle garden. *Polystichum tsus-simense* is attractive, and likes humid air.

Two or three plants are often enough to make a good effect. When they are firmly in place, water them until the

Figure 20

Ted Budlong

Miniature plants in minature containers are shown here. The plant on the glass table is growing in a toothpaste tube cap, which gives an index of size. It is a very young clover. The long planter at the left contains Helxine soleirolii and the other long planter holds sedum. The rubber plant, actually a lemon seedling, is in a floor planter which was made by turning a dollhouse lampshade upside down and waterproofing it. The picture of Great-Uncle Henry was contributed by the photographer.

soil is moist but not soggy, and put the lid on them.

After the first bottle garden is completed, and you are used to working inside a bottle without three hands, you can plan more complicated effects. Terrarium plants that like a closed container should also be checked to be sure they are slow-growing.

A more unusual project than a bottle garden is a planted branch to go against a wall (Figure 19). This should be a tree branch that has an interesting line, with several smaller branches leading off from it.

The first part of this project obviously is a walk in the woods, or a visit to a friend well supplied with trees who will donate a branch. A useful portion of a tree limb sometimes will be blown down in a storm, but this is too much luck to be expected.

The second step is to show your branch to a relative or a friend with a saw, and explain how you need it cut. You might have a rough sketch, showing how the branch will look after trimming, to make sure of a satisfactory final design, and also to provide guidelines for the sawing. The small secondary branches should be cut off at different lengths, according to how the composition is worked out, but most of them will be cut fairly close to the main branch so it will dominate.

In imagining the final effect, consider that the branch may be hung on the wall at a slant or level. It may lift sharply from the severed end upward; it may slant more gradually; it may be forked in large or small proportion, and thus the main limb be level. This positioning will help a decision as to length of remaining small portions of the side branches. Since screw eyes will be set in the branch eventually, for hanging, you may want to do this at an early stage, attach wire, and experiment with the branch on a wall. You may also want to compare an end branch and a section cut from the middle of a long limb because of its helpful shape.

Hang or stand the branch somewhere to wait and dry out a bit, while you advance on the next stage of the project. Meanwhile, put a small box nearby to collect important small bits of bark that may get knocked off the branch, that you'll want to reattach later.

You are going to settle small plants in the forks between main branch and side branches, and in pockets cut out with a hole saw or attached at the back. So depending on the size of the branch and the sketch design of the final effect you want, start collecting the plants. The largest plant might be chosen first. If you can find a staghorn fern small enough for the arrangement, this is an epiphyte or air plant, and should do well here. Small cushions of moss can be added to the collection.

Areas of planting depend on the individual branch, which may have a deep hollow space at one fork, a large empty knothole, a twist that can be used with backing for a planting pocket. Other pockets can be whittled or sawed out, in chosen positions.

Pockets will be filled with osmunda or peat moss or fir bark chips, and occasionally soil. They will have varying depths. Their effect is better than wiring plants to the branch.

Small bromeliads do well in a branch garden. Very small ferns can be found for pockets, but these will usually need attentive watering. Other epiphytic ferns besides the staghorn include the golden polypody and the hare's foot fern.

Settle for a long planting period, while you experiment with plants in different arrangements, and order plants for special effects. As you get them, check what their preferences are for water and nutrient. You will probably do a lot of misting, and when the branch is in place on the wall, you may want to waterproof a section of wall as mentioned for wall trellises in Chapter 4. Select plants for sun or shade, according to where the branch will hang.

The branch garden will need attention, but it is unusual enough to be worth it. If you want more humidity for it, hang it over one of the groupings of long planter and screened pots on a tray of pebbles and water; the two might combine well for appearance also.

A simple project, in contrast to a branch garden, is making miniature hanging baskets, literally the size of a thimble or smaller. You can weave them quickly with wire. Take three lengths of wire, twist them together at the center, and then spread and bend them so they curve up U-shaped from the bottom joining. Leave two opposing wires long for the handle. Clip the others with wire cutters till they are the right height for your small basket; you can picture them as the ribs of the basket, spreading them to get the shape. Finer wire will circle around at the center and top, twisted once around each upright stronger wire in passing, so there will be a woven effect, the ends finally being twisted together, clipped and turned inside. Now you have a basket that will fit on a finger, with the two wires extending out from it. These two meet in a curve above the basket, and are bent down again, each to twine around the other wire till the basket edge is reached, so there is a loop of long handle of the twisted wire. The basket is packed with wet sphagnum moss, the moss shaped so it follows the outline of the basket but comes out sometimes between the wires. Nutrient is added to the moss, or a small hollow at the center filled with soil. A sedum tip goes in the basket, or a snatch of *Helxine soleirolii,* or any tiny vine or plant. These small baskets of course have to be watered daily.

Miniature hanging baskets go in the terrarium, to swing from a long twig. They also are a charming addition to the formal garden of a planter, hanging from their slim green poles, which are made of pieces of bamboo garden stake with a wired-on cross piece of the same material near the top, one arm longer than the other.

Indoor gardens have a place as a group project. Any of the larger gardens can be a family project, the waterfall garden, for example.

The smaller movable gardens are a focus of interest for a club or for an informal group of friends. Working on indoor gardens together is not only a shared interest, it is often a pooling of ideas and information. One person has an idea for a design, another has grown flowers that would be right for the planter and its future placement, another knows a new nursery that is starting a line of miniature plants. So a garden will be worked out jointly. Another time, each person might prefer to work out a separate small garden. And again, the group can work together on seasonal gardens and gifts.

A group can work efficiently to make a number of attractive gardens, for use in a community affair, a church bazaar or a school fair. These could be auctioned or sold, and make a most decorative booth.

A garden party, in a new sense, sets each guest composing the design for a garden. Inexpensive pottery containers, plants, and all the makings are set out down the length of a long table, near the center. Gardens grow into shape around this table, and at small side tables. Prizes for the most original garden, the garden with the best composition, can be a small misting spray, and miniature garden tools that come in plastic and in matching brass sets. And of course everyone has a garden to take home.

A group becoming interested in further possibilities for indoor gardens can specialize. Perhaps in miniature roses, perhaps miniature geraniums, whatever is decided upon. Concentration on ferns leads far from the usually seen varieties, and the indoor gardens profit. Some of the interesting ferns that might be investigated are the harts tongue fern, cliff-brakes, and dwarf blechnum ferns.

Group specialization can begin easily and gather momentum. Membership in a horticultural society, trips to botanic gardens and nurseries, reports on books dealing with the chosen specialty, all contribute to a good start.

14. Gardens for Children

GARDENS FOR CHILDREN MAY BE PURELY FOR FUN AND DIVERSION. They also can lead on to curiosity about growing plants from seeds, or the peculiar habits and needs of some plants. And they can be related to scientific experiments that catch the absorbed interest of older children and have multi-faceted results.

Gardens for younger children start sometimes with seeds or cuttings, sometimes with plants. If simple care of the garden, such as watering the plants without flooding them, giving feedings as needed, is explained from the point of view of the plants, there will be no flavor of chores about this. A little personalization of plants is useful here, as small children readily see the discomfort of standing for hours with their feet in water or missing meals.

A garden that makes a good starter for a younger child, with interesting plants that can take generous water while the matter of correct watering is getting under control, is a turtle swamp. For a container, an inexpensive terrarium can be made as described in Chapter 9, or four pieces of glass may be cut to fit the sides of a deep oblong pan, with the corners and top edges taped. A taped piece of glass for the top is useful for cold nights, or to retain moisture when the family is away for a weekend.

Some of the plants, moss, and accessories for this swamp garden, curls of bark, tiny logs, and lichens, could be collected on a treasure hunt near a lake or stream, or in the woods. This gives the child a personal identification with the garden from the start. Or a terrarium kit can be ordered, for basic supplies or for city dwellers without easy access to the country, that provides an array of attractive garden components from ferns and partridge-berry to driftwood and striped pipsissewa. The kit includes clumps of springy moss for the higher ground or slope of the garden, and live sphagnum moss for the swampy area.

Insect-eating plants that will also appreciate raw hamburger belong in this swamp garden. These, as well as the terrarium kit, may be ordered from Arthur Eames Allgrove. The Venus flytrap, northern pitcher plants, and huntsman's horn make an interesting appearance as well as having unusual eating habits.

The garden is prepared for planting as suggested in Chapter 9. An insulating wall of slate and heavy foil should be placed underground, separating the marshy section from the rocks and soil of higher ground. There should be a pool in the marsh, with pebbles and small bits of rock sloping up to ground level at one side, and a sizable chip floating on the water for use by the small turtle. A shallow bowl can be used for the pool, with some attention to keeping the pebbles in place; a simpler solution that allows the turtle an easy exit from the pool is to make a pool of Sakrete as described in Chapter 2, with one side sloping up for a turtle ramp.

The insulating wall permits heavier watering of the marsh area without too much seepage into the rest of the garden. A small marsh for pitcher plants is seen in the terrarium in Figure 13 at the front left corner, which is kept very damp without affecting nearby plants that prefer less water. Plants for both the marsh area and the higher ground are suggested in Chapter 5.

A small garden for a child's room can use some of the materials of the terrarium kit. Here is the place for the round fish bowl (Figure 21), which permits higher humidity, with a good view of all sides.

Figure 21

Ira Finke

This terrarium for a child can be covered part of the time. Some of the plants mentioned in Chapter 5 are used here: goldthread, partridge-berry, pipsissewa. There is a rattlesnake plantain, club moss, and lichen. Green moss makes a simple ground cover.

An open garden that has plants of interesting shapes and that does not need frequent watering is a desert scene. Plants for this are cacti and succulents chosen at the five-and-ten cent store, or at a garden center or nursery. Though the main part of the scene will be sandy stretches and stones with unusual cacti scattered about, there should be a corner for contrast.

This can be a hill, with small succulents and a bromeliad, the slope concealing insulating walls, so watering of this section will not affect the lower desert ground with its cacti. The bromeliad could be a zebra plant (Figure 8) to be watered infrequently at the roots, and placed at the top of the hill to control this, but with water put more often in the cup formed by the leaves.

Instead of a hill, an oasis could be used for contrast. A corner is set apart again by an insulating wall out of sight under the sand. Here are one or two small palms, grasses, and possibly a pool.

The matter of attention to proper watering of course varies with the individual child. For a child interested in this and other aspects of plant care, an open garden offers wide choices. It can start with seedlings; include vines that will climb a trellis; follow the design of a garden in one of the other chapters.

If seeds are to be used, hardy flowering plants like marigolds make a good beginning. Marigold seedlings are sturdy, which is important during the practice stage of transplanting when the child learns to place the seedlings firmly but not too tightly in the soil.

A few miniature plants give immediate personality to the garden. Some of these can be bought from a greenhouse, already budding, such as dwarf pinks and Johnny-jump-ups.

Plants with interesting characteristics are an important part of a child's garden. In addition to the insect-eating plants, there is the walking fern, that starts a new plant from the tip of a frond. There is the pick-a-back plant, with little plants formed at the base of its leaf stalks. The sensitive plant will curl its leaves at a touch. The telegraph plant got its common name from the curious movements of its leaflets. And the magic leaf, sometimes called air plant—*Kalanchoe pinnata*—hanging in the window above the garden, a single leaf pinned to the curtain, forms tiny plants along its edges (Figure 22). I have used eight of these leaves for an unusual mobile.

Figure 22

A Kalanchoe pinnata *leaf, with young plants growing from its edges.* Ted Budlong

A wind-chime garden has charm in spring and summer at a window of a child's room. As the center of the garden, one small wind-chime can be hung from a slim pole with an arm attached at the top. Or the little glass pieces can be separated, and combined again in smaller groups at two corners of the garden, to swing and chime together in the breeze.

The container for the open garden can be a small planter if space is restricted, or a flat made waterproof with a sheet of heavy plastic. To provide space for more plants and garden effects, an indoor window box can be set on brackets level with a windowsill.

One or two plants that need more precise care could be included here, such as miniature roses, with the main part of the garden planted with easily tended flowers: sweet alyssum, zinnias (the small Tom Thumb variety), miniature snap-dragons. One of the fast-spreading sedums makes easy ground cover, and edging with tendrils reaching outside the garden.

For older children there are endless variations of a how-it-happens garden. Here a few seeds are sacrificed, taken up at various stages of development, so the whole process from seed to seedling can be followed. Also some of the larger seeds, nasturtium for example, can be planted in a glass bowl, next to the glass, where they are visible as they open, sprout, put down roots.

This can be done with flowering plants, or with beans and other vegetables. Grapefruit, lemon, tangerine seeds are interesting to watch as they progress toward little trees for the garden.

If seeds are grown in a separate container, and selected strong seedlings moved to the indoor garden, there is opportunity for practice in transplanting and for planning a well-designed garden. Or seeds can be planted in different areas of the garden, to be moved and thinned out later.

Home gardens can be linked with school projects. As children progress in elementary school, of course, this becomes more diversified. Sometimes it will mean experiments at home that tie in with scientific studies at school. Sometimes it will mean knowledgeable care of a more interesting garden, because of information gained at school.

The scientific approach to the area of growing things that is offered many of the older children at school, does more than deepen specific knowledge. It interests children in doing their own thinking; like a mystery story, it shows that a "why" may lead on to a "how," with an experiment providing clues. It takes the youthful curse off rules and precise method when a plant is shown responding to correct care. And experiments that prove what growing plants really need are apt to pay off in better garden-making.

This aspect of early science courses, in which children develop a habit of finding their own answers and gaining knowledge through their own experiments, instead of memorizing an adult's answer, is on the upswing in this country.

As it relates to plants, it covers such things as how plants get and use water, minerals, carbon dioxide, sunlight.

When such courses are given in the schools of a community, there is a tie-in for garden-minded parents and garden clubs. When they are not yet given, some of the experiments may be done at home, with interest for adults as well as children, and profit for the children's gardens. Books in this connection include: *Science You Can Use* and *Science in Action*, both by George K. Stone with Lucy W. Stephenson; also *Projects: Botany*, by Doris M. Stone.

A suggested experiment in the second book, with radish seeds planted in two pots, and one of the pots kept covered so no light is admitted, illustrates in ten days the importance of light, by the contrasting condition of seedlings in the two pots. Similar experiments can show the importance of proper feeding, proper watering. This has far better results with the young gardener than saying "do this." And further experiments lead on to further knowledge, as well as to a respect for the right method that gets the right results.

Gardens for children profit from simple as well as complex experiments that catch at interest and curiosity, and provide information pleasurably. Younger children, who might find the regular watering of a garden dull if it is set as a task, get the point quickly if two small gardens are planted as twins, one watered and the other left dry with the plants curling and browning.

When there are indoor gardens in the house, whether a more elaborate waterfall garden or a simple window planter, children sometimes want to share in the interest with gardens of their own, and sometimes want to compete. There can be group projects, scouting projects, a garden planned to suit the child's room, or one that fits a child's special interest.

Gardens planted when snow is still on the ground and seeds need the indoor warmth will give flowers and vegetables an early start when transplanted in warm weather. Gardens started in the fall provide flowers and bright foliage for winter months. Gardens also can be a year-round concern, the contents changing gradually from time to time for continued interest.

The indoor garden is a personal possession for the child, set apart in its container, responding visibly to care. Some of its contents should have been started personally—the child's own plants, from seed to flower.

15. *Doors to More Gardens*

INDOOR GARDENS HAVE A WAY OF LEADING ON TO FURTHER provocative territories, some new, some known but not yet fully explored. Possibilities wait like half-opened doors, and one of these is specialization.

Areas of specialization are as beguiling as a flower show. There is also the lure of competition with a friend who is concentrating on miniature geraniums, miniature roses. Better, one can take a step off the well-planted path. For example, there are many inducements for specializing in gesneriads, which are taken up in detail in Chapter 16.

Bonsai culture is a territory that has its own fascination. This need not mean tiny trees that are several hundred years old and correspondingly expensive. There are easier approaches.

In addition to naturally dwarfed trees, there are small trees to be trained over a period of time to the desired shape. Also seedlings may be used, pinched back at an early stage and trained. For details of technique, there are lectures, classes, and books.

Apart from the precise boundaries of bonsai culture, there

are many uses for miniature trees in indoor gardens. These may be planted in a relatively small pot at first to discourage root growth, and be pruned and trained as with bonsai, or allowed to take their own way. They may be used as part of a landscape, or in a small garden that features them. The four-year-old tree in Figure 23 is planted in a larger container than would be used for bonsai, in proportion to the size; combined with a small rock and vine, it takes its place as a miniature tree in a miniature scene.

A territory that has special value for those living in apartments or who have problems with sunlight and limited space is the use of fluorescent lighting. Most house plants respond well to this in both growth and bloom, and seedlings are encouraged.

Better results are gained from deciding on the plants to be used in a garden with fluorescent lighting, and the effect desired in a room from the decorative point of view—and then working out the lighting. Combinations of fluorescent tubes, reflector and holder should be considered, and also the possibility of an automatic timer. A special stand can be made to hold the tubes if there is a special purpose. My own stand was made by combining a sturdy base, on casters; a pole with a long arm; and a large workbench hood. It can be moved easily from one garden to another. Plants have been cheered and heartened by the use of an ordinary fluorescent desk lamp. But if new lighting is being added, there are the tubes which are especially for use with plants.

Fluorescent lights not only have their place with the floor garden in a dark corner and the bookcase shelf adapted to flowers, they also permit gardening in the basement or the pantry cupboard. There can be a place for cuttings and seedlings, apart from the gardens to which they will move later.

In working out arrangements of planters and fluorescent lights, heavy extension cords should be used, with the connections covered as a protection against water. The light tubes should be at least within a foot of the plants for best results.

Plants may be satisfactorily grown under fluorescent light, which opens up any part of the apartment or house for them.

Figure 23

A four-year-old miniature spruce, Picea glauca conica

Ted Budlong

Or the lighting can be used several hours a day for plants that get daylight but not enough sunlight. Specific plants might get ten hours of fluorescent light a day for sturdy growth and more rapid bloom. It depends on the plants, the location, and the purpose.

An area that deserves attention is that of containers. There are some attractive containers on the market, but not enough to fill all needs. Also an original container is apt to suit better the garden that is being planted and the room where it will stand.

Sometimes this means shopping and searching, not always specifically for a planter, but for something that will serve well as a planter. This may be a soup tureen, as mentioned in Chapter 6; a basket of woven wood strips that can be fitted with a watertight lining; the stone crock that your great-grandmother used for keeping pickles. With the desired size in mind, and the general effect that's wanted, a little looking usually produces something more interesting than a commercial container.

Making a planter ensures that it will have the precise size and character you want. You may like to work in clay, metal, or wood. You may want a new project for a rainy day, and start experimenting.

If you like the designing but not the making, then show your sketch and notes to a carpenter, tinsmith, or that friend who has taken up ceramics. Exact measurements are important—for instance, to make sure of good depth for pebbles if you aren't using drainage holes. If you are ordering a wooden planter, make sure it is caulked and treated with rot preventative; or a metal liner may be preferred. And while you order a wooden planter, you might want to include an indoor window box, or a propagating box to fit a special space.

Propagation is interesting in itself, and a steady source of plants for the gardens. Propagation by seeds may be done handily in a seed pan, or in flowerpots or baking pans. There must be the usual drainage layer of pebbles or crock. It is easier to buy soil, but outdoor garden earth can be sterilized and sifted. Soil should be moist, and seeds scattered on the surface, covered with soil as appropriate to their type, and lightly tamped down. Pans or pots are then covered with a pane of glass or with plastic till the seeds germinate, after which fresh air is important, and the seedlings should move gradually to good light. The soil should be kept moist throughout.

The other means of propagation, vegetative, includes several methods, of which two of the simplest are by the use of division and cuttings. Division, as is done with African violets, is a matter of careful separation. Cuttings or slips of some plants may be started in water; others may be planted directly in the garden they are intended for, but the majority of cuttings benefit from a period in very moist, warm air. This moist climate is provided by a propagating box, which can be bought or made; by a terrarium; by the ubiquitous ancient aquarium with a cover; or a glass jar placed over each cutting.

A variety of mediums are used for cuttings: a mixture of soil and sand, sand alone, or equal parts of sand and peat moss. Stem cuttings are fitted firmly into the sand or other medium. Leaf cuttings, such as those of streptocarpus or rex begonia, with the main veins cut across on the under side, can be placed flat on the sand right side up with stem inserted, and weighted or pegged there. The propagating box or other covered container should be aired daily and checked so that the sand continues moist.

Driftwood combines well with indoor gardens. No doubt you have seen arrangements of driftwood with dried grasses, seed pods, and the like, or made these. Some of the values gained by these patterns can be found in combining driftwood and miniature plants, or ferns and larger plants. There is the pleasure of composition, the completed design, and the added contribution of living plants and flowers.

Sometimes driftwood is subordinated, partly hidden by plants, as it breaks a line that is too regular, as in Figure 25. Or the emphasis can be on an unusually shaped piece of wood, with its lines followed or balanced by one or two plants.

One of the most interesting possibilities to be explored, through one of these garden doors, is the development of new varieties of plants, of plants with new characteristics, with flowers of a new shape or color. This can mean the excitement of discovery or the reward for patient work. It means a highly personal garden that contains a plant that is new—and your own.

This particular territory does not demand training in its skills. It needs interest and detailed knowledge, a knowledge that can be obtained, for example, from John James' book on the creation of new flowers and plants, listed among Suggested Books.

Two things combine well here—specialization and the development of new plants. As you start to specialize, you will want to know the recognized members of the selected plant family, and the plants of the species of that family that attract you most. As interest in them grows, it often leads to an interest in hybridization.

Specialization is a personal thing, of course, apt to evolve of itself, whether in stamp collecting, antiques, or the flowers for indoor gardens. If it is taken slowly, after a general survey, it is apt to be lasting.

There is one's subjective reaction, which is basic in choosing what to specialize in. There is the factor of the space available. There is the matter of the kind of gardens wanted for different rooms, hanging baskets or terrariums or large open planters, and the kind of plants that will be featured well in these rooms and gardens.

And before making a final decision, there is the important point of specializing in something that has not been done widely and thoroughly already. It is more fun to make one's specialty an area in which there are plants and flowers less often seen, sometimes new to this country. Also, unusual indoor gardens result.

Specialization doesn't mean something difficult, or that advance knowledge is needed. Starting with a selection of plants that pleases you, with a cultural handbook, with membership in an appropriate society that gives access to information and shared interest, you are well on your way.

16. Gesneriad Gardens

GESNERIADS HAVE BEEN MENTIONED IN OTHER CHAPTERS, AMONG
the plantings for open gardens and terrariums. They have been
suggested for specialization. And when they are featured, in
differing combinations, they provide striking and individual
indoor gardens.

A wide selection is offered by the gesneria family—a tropical
largesse, ranging from bright drama in leaves and flowers of
varying sizes, to the piquant effect of ultra-miniature flowering
plants. They have the added interest that they originated in
far places: tropical forests, mountains as distant as the Hima-
layas, locations as varied as Africa, South America, Malaya,
Europe, and islands of the Pacific.

The genealogy of gesneriaceae is apt to be surprising. Not
only have some members of the family been misnamed in
common usage, but others have become familiar under a
popular name, more or less as orphans without lineage. One
meets unexpected gesneriad relatives, hybrids or recent ar-
rivals from foreign parts, the constantly expanding cultivars
and varieties that give the group its quality of newness—then
one sees a saintpaulia and recalls that the African violet has
been around for quite a while.

African violets have their loyal group of aficionados. But other gesneriads, a second step off that previously mentioned well-planted path, offer the lure of the unfamiliar, and of course vastly wider range in flowers and leafage.

In deciding on a choice of plants for an indoor garden, it's a help to see some of them at nurseries or botanic gardens, to go through color plates of books and catalogs. There is incidentally the danger of a sort of pleasant horticultural indigestion, from wanting too many of them at once. They are apt to have a shape, color, quality that gets a triple-take.

"What's that?" is the first reaction to unfamiliar scarlet flowers spilling out lushly, or to foliage that seems purple velvet laid on green velvet. "I want that" is the immediate next reaction.

A garden stressing gesneriads may start with a single species, but often interest fans out more widely. And then, gradually, one gains familiarity with the botanical names. In a great many cases there are no popular names. Thus anyone unfamiliar with gesneriads might be slightly daunted by the accumulation of botanical names, but this situation is bridged by the fact that selection for one's own garden may start as simply and progress as slowly as desired. For example, one starts with a single genus of the family, perhaps two or three species or subspecies. Incidentally, the new gesneriad species are continually being discovered in the wild and introduced to cultivation. Also, plant breeders and specialist growers of gesneriads are introducing fascinating new hybrids, sports, and other cultivars that originated in their gardens.

Note the botanical names on a reference card that can stay out of sight in a drawer, while you get acquainted with your plants. You will perhaps think of them at first by some descriptive tag or short name of your own. And conversational use of the botanical names can come along naturally later; just as often there is a period after meeting someone when you are poised between the first name or formal title, and skip the whole matter or say "you".

Those preferring the precise names from the start can wander lightheartedly through the catalogs and culture books. They may note en route that the two main subdivisions of gesneriads divide into six main categories. Of these, three that contain some of the best types for the indoor garden are differentiated by three characteristics: those having tubers, those with fibrous roots, and those with underground scaly rhizomes. The rhizomes—a means of propagation—are produced at the base of the stem and resemble a small longish cone.

In narrowing down choices for the garden from the array of interesting gesneriads, one factor is whether the container will be open or a terrarium-type used for more humidity. Also, though most species like the same lighting, with sunlight in cooler seasons and screened sunlight in summer, some accept a northern window. Other points of culture, discussed later, are similar for most plants.

Recommendations follow of a dozen examples of gesneriads, according to the type of indoor garden. These are suggested by Paul Arnold as gesneriads most likely to succeed without expert care. Mr. Arnold is a specialist *par excellence* in gesneriads, who has introduced many new plants, and who has the largest collection in the world of *Achimenes* varieties.

For a window garden: *Episcia,* miniature *Sinningia, Streptocarpus* and trailers like *Columnea*

For a garden with fluorescent lighting: *Episcia, Sinningia, Rechsteineria, Smithiantha*

For the high humidity of a terrarium: *Boea, Episcia, Koellikeria, Sinningia pusilla*

The adaptable *Episcia* mentioned for all three locations is shown in Figure 3, where the creamy pattern of *E.* 'Tricolor' can be seen at the lower right, and in Figures 6 and 25. Mr. Arnold suggests that any gesneriad miniature will do best in the humidity of a terrarium. Gesneriads in general appreciate moist air. In the terrarium shown in Figure 13, *Achimenes andrieuxii* is flowering at the right front corner; the small cushioned leaves of *Streptocarpus saxorum* rise on long stems behind it; at the front center are the purple and green leaves of *Smithiantha zebrina* 'Little One,' brilliantly in bloom. The tiny flowers of *Sinningia pusilla* are seen in both terrariums. In the terrarium in Figure 14, *Columnea* 'Joy' is in bloom

Figure 24

Donald H. Clark

For a fall effect, Sinningia speciosa *blooms above peaches and a spray of dog-wood.*

Figure 25

Donald H. Clark
Ira Finke

Something is always budding or blooming in the gesneriad garden, described in this chapter. In the upper photograph, Streptocarpus rexii *is in bud at the center,* Columnea 'Joy' *at the far left, and* Sinningia pusilla *is in flower at the center edge. In the lower photograph, taken a month later,* Rechsteineria cardinalis *is in bloom. The leaves, with their differing texture and color, have their own interest.*

at the left, with a budding *Koellikeria erinoides* in front of it; *Sinningia concinna* flowers at the right front, next to S. *pusilla*, and a hybrid *Sinningia* 'Bright Eyes' above the pool.

For an open planter, some selections are shown in Figure 25. Among them are the velvety foliage of *Kohleria* 'Longwood'; *Rechsteineria leucotricha* with its leaves set in whorls; *R. cardinalis*, lower and more compact; *Streptocarpus rexii* with a bud lifting from low flat leaves. In the lower photograph *R. cardinalis* is in bloom.

Sinningia speciosa, familiar to some as florist's gloxinia, is shown in the white flowers of the room-divider planter, Figure 4. Also, in another color, in the grouping of Figure 24.

Gesneriad miniatures can be very small indeed. They live in a terrarium, or in their own separate terrarium-type container, most easily; or in open gardens, with careful attention.

For some years *Sinningia pusilla* was known as the smallest gesneriad (Figure 27). More recently, *Phinea multiflora* (Figure 26), with a still smaller flower, was brought to this country by Harold E. Moore, Jr., whose definitive book on gesneriads is listed with Suggested Books.

A new import, not as yet offered for sale in this country at this time of writing, is *Sinningia hirsuta*. This should be noted when available; it blooms readily, is of dwarf size, has the long hairs on leaves and stem indicated in its name, and is generally attractive.

Returning to familiar gesneriads, there are some that have become known under other names than their true ones. There is not only the African violet, but also the lipstick plant—*Aeschynanthus*. And the florists' gloxinias mentioned above are actually *Sinningia speciosa*, the name *Gloxinia* belonging to another genus.

The error of the miscalled gloxinias became widespread, so that the name was accepted in its horticultural usage. Now this confusion is being addressed. The name of the American Gloxinia Society was changed in the summer of 1966 to the American Gloxinia and Gesneriad Society.

Culture is basically the same for most gesneriads, with the fact noted that different ones prefer different locations. Though some will take a north window, most need some sunlight. As mentioned, this means direct sun except in summer, when there should be some screening of the light. Fluorescent light can be substituted for sunlight.

Humidity is an important factor. If small gesneriads are not grown in terrariums, there should be a humidifying water-container hung behind a radiator, or other device used so the air won't be too dry in indoor heating during northern winters. If an arrangement is used with a long planter in front and pots concealed behind, these can be on a pebble-and-water tray.

Figure 26

Ted Budlong

Phinea multiflora, *with the smallest flower of the gesneriads, is shown here temporarily residing in a jigger glass, to give the proportions.*

Figure 27

Ted Budlong

Sinningia pusilla, in an inch-and-a-quarter pot, has one of its flowers reflected in the crystal dish.

Misting with a fine spray is now approved. It was once questioned as the cause of leaf spotting, but the rule now is that no ill effects occur when the water is within ten degrees of room temperature. I keep a long-nosed watering can filled, so the water is always at room temperature, and smaller watering pots and sprays can be filled from this. There should be fresh air, though not cold drafts. When a terrarium is used, the top should be partially or completely off part of the time, depending on climate and heating conditions.

Soil should be screened and sterilized. An easy choice is commercial African violet mix. It should stay lightly moist, and watering as with misting should be done with water at room temperature.

When soil is used, feeding once a month is sufficient. When miniatures are grown in sphagnum moss, feeding should be given every two weeks. The general rule is a tablespoon per gallon, of plant food such as Rapid Gro, for occasional feeding. Some growers use very dilute liquid fertilizer every time they water the plants, about a fifth of a teaspoon per gallon of water.

Gesneriads are a notable success for indoor gardens because of their great variety, their effectiveness, and the relative ease of caring for them. There are gesneriads for large planters, for table-size open planters and scenes such as the waterfall garden, and accents for terrariums such as the busily blooming sinningias in the terrariums illustrated. They can be featured alone in an appropriate container, or used in hanging baskets. Wherever they are, they add interesting foliage and flowers.

Start with two or three. Start even with one. And sooner or later, plant by irresistible plant, there will be a gesneriad garden.

Selected List of Suppliers

Alberts and Merkel Bros., Inc.
P.O. Box 537
Boynton Beach, Fla. 33435

orchids and other tropicals
catalog, $.50

Alpenglow Gardens
13328 King George Highway
North Surrey
British Columbia, Canada

evergreens
alpines
shrubs

Arthur Eames Allgrove
N. Wilmington, Mass. 01887

terrarium plants
woodland plants
supplies
catalog, $.25

Buell's Greenhouses
Eastford, Conn. 06242

gesneriads
catalog, $1

Michael J. Kartuz
92 Chestnut St.
Wilmington, Mass. 01887

gesneriad specialties
begonias

Mayfair Nurseries
R.D. 2
Nichols, N. Y. 13812

dwarf conifers
dwarf shrubs

Merry Gardens
Camden, Maine 04843

house plants
bromeliads
miniatures
catalog, $.50

* It is suggested that when catalog is free, postage be enclosed.

Nicholas Orlando
Mount Kisco, N. Y. 10507

room divider with planter

Peter Pauls Nurseries
R.D. 4
Canandaigua, N. Y. 14424

bonsai
terrarium plants
supplies

Roehrs Exotic Nurseries
Rutherford, N. J. 07070

house plants
exotics
catalog, $.25

Harry E. Saier
Dimondale, Mich. 48821

seeds
catalog, $.50

Thompson and Morgan
(Ipswich) Ltd.
Ipswich, England

seeds

Tiny Trees Nursery Co.
5212 N. Peck Rd.
El Monte, Calif. 91732

bonsai
catalog, $.10

Tool Shed Herb Nursery
Salem Center
Purdy's Station, New York 10578

herbs
catalog, $.25

Thomas M. Wood
Constantia, N. Y. 13044

woodland plants

Suggested Books

American Home Editors and Staff, *The American Home Garden Book and Plant Encyclopedia,* New York, Lippincott, 1963.

Ashberry, Anne, *Miniature Gardens* (English Gardens in Miniature), London, C. Arthur Pearson, Ltd., 1951.

Bailey, L. H. and E. Z., compilers, *Hortus Second: A Concise Dictionary of Gardening,* New York, Macmillan, 1941.

Brandon, Dorothy, and Scheider, Alfred F., *The Max Schling Book of Indoor Gardening,* New York, Ivan Obolensky, 1963.

Brilmayer, Bernice, *All About Miniature Plants and Gardens, Indoors and Out,* New York, Doubleday, 1953.

Brooklyn Botanic Garden, Handbooks on *Gardening in Containers* and other subjects, Brooklyn 25, New York.

Cathey, Henry M., *Indoor Garden for Decorative Plants,* Washington, U. S. Government Printing Office, 1965.

Cherry, Elaine C., *Fluorescent Light Gardening,* Princeton, Van Nostrand, 1965

Everett, T. H., *How to Grow Beautiful House Plants,* New York, Arco, 1965.

Foster, F. Gordon, *The Gardener's Fern Book,* Princeton, Van Nostrand, 1964.

Free, Montague, *All About House Plants,* New York, Doubleday, 1946.

Graf, Alfred Byrd, *Exotica 3: Pictorial Cyclopedia of Exotic Plants,* Rutherford, N.J., Roehrs Co., 1963.

Greene, Wilhelmina F., and Blomquist, Hugo L., *Flowers of the South,* Chapel Hill, University of North Carolina Press, 1953.

Ishimoto, Tatsuo, *A Treasury of Driftwood Arrangements*, New York, Crown, 1962.

James, John, *Create New Flowers and Plants—Indoors and Out*, New York, Doubleday, 1964.

Kartus, Michael J., and Clayberg, Carl D., *Cultural Handbook: Gloxinias and Other Gesneriads*, Eastford, Conn., The Gloxinia and Gesneriad Society.

McDonald, Elvin, *Miniature Plants for Home and Greenhouse*, Princeton, Van Nostrand, 1962.

Moore, Harold E., Jr., *African Violets, Gloxinias and Their Relatives—A Guide to the Cultivated Gesneriads*, New York, Macmillan, 1957.

Padilla, Victoria, editor, *Bromeliads in Color and their Culture*, Los Angeles, Cal., The Bromelian Society, 1966.

Rickett, Harold W., *Botany for Gardeners*, New York, Macmillan, 1957.

Stowell, Jerald P., *Bonsai Indoors and Out*, Princeton, Van Nostrand, 1966.

Sunset Books and Magazine Editorial Staffs, *Gardening in Containers*, Menlo Park, Calif., Lane Magazine and Book Co., 1959.

Taylor, Norman, editor, *Taylor's Encyclopedia of Gardening*, Boston, Houghton Mifflin Co., 1961.

Index

Index

Pluto, 121
Plywood planters, 18–20
Pole lamps, vines on, 28–29
Polystichum tsus-simense, 48
  in bottle gardens, 128
  in rock gardens, 80
Pools, 20
  in rock gardens, 82
Portulacas, 109
  curative powers of, 119
Pot marjoram (*Origanum
    onites*), 70
Potted plants, 26, 97–98
  See also House plants
Primrose, 101
  fairies and, 119
  in salads, 123
Projects, 124–33
  bottle gardens as, 127–29
  gifts as, 124–27
  group, 132–33
  planted branch as, 129–31
Projects: Botany (Doris Stone),
    140
Propagation, 145–46
Pteris ensiformis evergemiensis,
    48
Pussy-toes (*Antennaria*), 82

Radiators, gardens on, 27–28
Ragwort, 119
Rainbow bush, 64
Rapid Gro, 154
Rechsteineria, 150
  cardinalis, 151
  leucotricha, 151
'Red Imp,' 63
Rhizomatous begonias, 62
Rhododendron, 32
Rock fern, 48
Rock gardens, 33, 74–83
  choosing rocks for, 74–76
  grottoes in, 81

landscaping, 76–78, 81–83
  planting, 78–81
Rocks
  insulating walls of, 13
  lichened, 22, 52
  waterfall gardens and, 20–22
Room dividers, 24
  gardens and, 26–27, 34
Rosary vines, 60, 64
Rose tree, 101
Rosemary, 69, 70
  magical properties of, 120
Roses
  jelly of, 123
  miniature, 62–63, 81
    'Baby Bunting,' 63
    'Bo-peep,' 63
    'Miss Muffet,' 63
    'Pixie Gold,' 63
    'Red Imp,' 63
    'Tom Thumb,' 63
  moisture for, 62–63
  in terrariums, 115–16
Rot preventive, 20
Rotation of plants, 97–99
Rowen, 118
Rubber plant, 99

Sage, 70
  preserved flowers of, 123
Saint-John's-wort (fairy horse),
    120
Saintpaulia (African violet),
    104–05
  in desk planters, 33
  division and, 146
  specialization and, 148–49
  for window screens, 40
Sakrete, 20, 21
Salads, herbs for, 68–69
Sand-dollars, 64
Sansevieria trifasciata, 99
  hahni, 99

WARE TORREY BUDLONG was described in Harper's *The Writer's Book* (for which she wrote a chapter) as follows: "Ware Torrey Budlong came to writing by way of newspaper work. Beginning as a syndicated feature writer, she moved on to positions as Washington correspondent, book review columnist of the Associated Press, and special foreign correspondent. Her fiction writing started with a group of mystery novels written under a pseudonym. Her short stories have been published in *The Saturday Evening Post,* other general magazines, women's magazines, British publications, and translated into half a dozen foreign languages."

Mrs. Budlong's articles appear in national magazines. Her published works include sixteen hard-cover and paperback books. Scheduled for publication are books by Mrs. Budlong in the areas of plant performance and plant physiology.

The author's interest in horticultural matters was influenced by the work of her great-great uncle, the botanist John Torrey. Mrs. Budlong is a member of the Poetry Society of America, the Horticultural Society of New York, the American Gloxinia and Gesneriad Society, the American Gesneria Society, and the New York Botanical Garden.

INDOOR GARDENS was set in type by the Harry Sweetman Typesetting Corportion, South Hackensack, New Jersey. The text is set in Caledonia.

A HAWTHORN BOOK